WORLD AFFAIRS SINCE 1919

World Affairs Since 1919

VERSAILLES TO THE KOREAN TRUCE JULY 1953

by

PETER WALES M.A., B.Sc. (ECON.)

Diploma in Social Studies

LONDON

METHUEN AND CO LTD

36 ESSEX STREET · STRAND · WC2

First published June 5th, 1958
Reprinted 1960 and 1962
© 1958 by Peter Wales
Printed in Great Britain
by Cox and Wyman Ltd, Fakenham

TO
MY WIFE
AND
PARENTS

1·3

CATALOGUE NO.
(BEST) 2/6033/1
(SCHOOL) 2/8161/6

FOREWORD

This book covers the history of world affairs from the Treaty of Versailles to the Korean Truce of July 1953. My aim has been to give the reader the background knowledge needed to interpret intelligently the headlines in his daily newspaper. The study of the recent history of important countries, and of their relations with each other, should be an important part of the education of all citizens in a democracy, and this book has been written because of the need for an introductory account in one volume of world affairs from the end of the first World War to recent events.

In a book of this size the major problem was obviously one of selection. South American affairs during this period, for instance, have not been considered of enough world importance to merit inclusion.[1] An adequate knowledge of political geography is essential for any fruitful reading of history and several political maps have been included. Important parts of the book are devoted to analysing the political philosophies of Communism and Fascism, the two chief totalitarian challenges in our time to democracy. Numerous biographical outlines of important figures of modern history have also been added. Essay questions can be found at the end of the book for the use of readers studying for examinations, and in answering these students should consult for further reading the lists at the ends of chapters.

I wish to take this opportunity to thank my wife for her constant encouragement, and also Flying Officer Jim Lloyd for his kindness in typing the final manuscript.

---

[1] Some account of South American affairs in the 'thirties can be found in G. M. Gathorne-Hardy's *A Short History of International Affairs 1920–1939.* Royal Institute of International Affairs, 1950.

CONTENTS

Contents

MAPS

[1] From L. C. B. Seaman's *From Vienna to Versailles* (Methuen: 1955).
[2] From G. E. Kirk's *A Short History of the Middle East* (Methuen: 1957).
[3] From D. C. Somervell's *Modern Europe, 1871–1950* (Methuen: 1953).
[4] From D. C. Somervell's *Modern Britain, 1870–1950* (Methuen: 1952).
[5] From Andrew Boyd's *An Atlas of World Affairs* (Methuen: 1957).

TIME CHART

MAJOR EVENTS 1919-1953

YEAR	EVENTS
1919	Treaty of Versailles League of Nations begins its work Civil war in Russia
1920	United States Senate votes against joining League
1921	French sign mutual security pact with Poland Washington Conference
1922	Treaty of Rapallo Mussolini seizes power in Italy
1924	Lenin dies—Stalin begins his rise to absolute power in Russia
1926	General Strike in Britain Germany admitted to League
1928	First Soviet Five-Year Plan
1929	Slump in U.S.A.—eventually spreads to all industrial countries Stalin exiles Trotsky
1931	National government formed in Britain to tackle slump Japan occupies Manchuria
1932	Roosevelt elected President on New Deal ticket
1933	Hitler becomes German Chancellor
1934	Anti-Republican riots in Paris
1936	German troops enter Rhineland Spanish Civil War begins
1937	Japan attacks China

Time Chart

1938   Germany occupies Austria
Munich meeting—Sudetenland given to Germany

1939   Germany occupies rest of Czechoslovakia
Russo-German non-aggression pact
Germany attacks Poland—declaration of war by
    Britain and France

1940   Germany occupies Norway
Churchill becomes Prime Minister of Coalition govern-
    ment
German offensive in Low Countries and France
Dunkirk evacuation
Italy declares war against Britain and France
France surrenders
Battle of Britain

1941   Wavell defeats Italians in Libya
Italian East Africa and Abyssinia cleared of enemy
Italy attacks Greece
Germany gains control of all Balkans
Germany attacks Russia
Atlantic Charter published
Pearl Harbour—Japan joins Germany and Italy.
    United States joins Allies

1942   Japan occupies large area of Asia
German offensive in Russia
Battle of El Alamein—Rommel prevented from cap-
    turing Suez Canal

1943   Stalingrad—Von Paulus surrenders
Axis forces surrender in Tunisia
Mussolini overthrown—Italy surrenders
Allied bombing of Germany steadily increases
VI and VII rockets land in England

1944   Normandy landings
France liberated
German Ardennes offensive fails
Russians reach Germany

Time Chart

1945   Hitler dies in Berlin seige
      Germany surrenders
      Atom bombs dropped on Japan
      Japan surrenders
      United Nations Organization begins its work

1946   Economic crisis in Europe

1947   Marshall Plan
      Suspicions grow regarding Russian intentions

1948   Dominion status achieved by India, Pakistan and Ceylon
      Brussels Treaty
      Organization for European Economic Co-operation formed
      Tito breaks with the Cominform

1949   North Atlantic Treaty Organization formed
      Communists gain control of China

1950   Korean War begins

1953   Stalin dies
      End of Korean War

INTRODUCTION

There are few of us who, at some time or another, when reading ominous headlines about international relations in some daily newspaper have not said to ourselves, 'Oh, well, what is the use of worrying about it? After all, I can't do anything in any case.' Relations between the major countries in the world seem rarely to be as amicable as we would wish and it is tempting to ignore the depressing subject of world affairs and to devote our time to studying other subjects. Why is it important that we should take an interest in world affairs and attempt to learn all we can about the politics and economics of other countries?

The first reason why it is so important for all of us to know something about world affairs is that we are living in Britain in a political democracy and at the age of twenty-one we are allowed to vote in local and general elections. How this country is governed finally rests with the people and upon the way they vote to decide who shall have charge of their affairs. But as well as running home affairs our government also controls our relations with other countries, and it is obvious that we are not going to be good citizens unless we know something about other countries and relations with them.

It is important, then, for all citizens in a democracy to know something of world affairs so that the country can be sensibly directed in its foreign relations. But, as well as this, the study of world affairs can prove very interesting. Knowing more about other countries gives us a background that helps us to understand the daily happenings abroad reported in our newspapers. We become more interesting people to meet because we can speak and write intelligently about events of importance in the world. In thinking about possible solutions to the many problems of international relations today we shall also find that we are using our brains just as much as in any game of chess.

DIFFICULTIES OF STUDYING WORLD AFFAIRS

In trying to find out more about world affairs we find that the subject has a number of problems. Firstly, its vastness. We have already agreed that knowing something about world affairs is an essential part of the education of every citizen. When we come to study the subject, however, we find it difficult to know where to begin in trying to build up our knowledge about other countries and about international relations. Our problem with the subject for a start is the selection of what is important to study from what is not. It is impossible for any of us to be experts on the affairs of every important country in the world and on all the major problems of international affairs. What we have got to try and achieve by wide reading and discussion with others interested in world affairs is a broad appreciation of the political and economic happenings of our time which have been mainly responsible for shaping the world we live in today. We have got to distinguish what is significant from what is not.

The next major difficulty we find with the subject is obtaining reliable sources of information about foreign countries and international relations. Many books written about world affairs are propagandist rather than carefully written books trying to discover the truth. Much of the official information and statistics given out by governments in dictatorships is also very unreliable. We must, then, when discussing subjects to do with world affairs always be careful to obtain reliable information on which to base our views.

A third problem, which sociologists—the people who attempt to study human society as carefully, objectively and scientifically as chemists and physicists study their subjects—have called the problem of ethno-centrism is also involved in a study of world affairs. By ethno-centrism we mean the assumption instinctively made by many people that the institutions and customs in their own country are right and where other countries differ from these ways of doing things they are wrong. Now, while we feel that our democratic way of life in the western part of the world is superior to the way of life enjoyed by many people elsewhere, we must always be careful to remember that other parts of the world have been affected by many factors peculiar to them and that some of their institutions different from our own may suit their local conditions. We need not go to the other extreme and take the view that ours is the best of all possible worlds and never criticise the ways of life of other countries. Finally the ways in which different societies organize themselves have to be looked at in terms of the happiness and well-being of the people living in them. In looking at other countries, however, we must take something of a relative view and bear in mind the particular local circumstances that have affected the development of different countries.

READING LIST

A student of world affairs can only keep abreast of contemporary events by a consistent and wide reading of newspapers and journals. *The Guardian* is particularly recommended for daily reading, but is not always available on the day of issue in all parts of the country. *The Times* and *Daily Telegraph* are also recommended. Weeklies which include many well documented articles on current events include *The Spectator*, *The Economist* (particularly good for its American Section) and *The New Statesman*. *The Political Science Quarterly* also contains well written articles by experts in the field of international relations.

Any teacher of world affairs is advised to check the *Radio Times* each week for programmes suitable for classes. Many interesting talks on other countries are given in the Schools' Education Broadcasts.

Introduction

Most foreign embassies in London contain Information Sections whose job it is to supply literature and films to British people interested in the country concerned. A particularly helpful organization is the United States Information Service at 5, Grosvenor Square, London W.1. The U.S. Information Service will supply pamphlets to schools and students studying American affairs, and will also consider the loan of films. A booklet on the work of the Service may be obtained on application. Particularly useful booklets obtainable from the Service include, *Facts about The United States*, *A Government by the People* (an introduction to the American system of government), and *The Negro in American life*.

GENERAL STUDIES

An Introduction to World Politics, W. Friedman (Macmillan).

World History since 1914, D. Thomson (Home University Library).

A Short History of International Affairs 1920–1939, G. M. Gathorne-Hardy (Royal Institute of International Affairs).

International Relations between The Two World Wars 1919–1939 E. H. Carr (Macmillan).

Modern Europe 1871–1950, D. C. Somervell (Methuen).

An Atlas of World Affairs, A. Boyd (Methuen).

Chapter One

THE PEACE SETTLEMENT 1919-1923

The direction taken by international affairs since the First
World War was largely conditioned by the provisions of the
various peace treaties signed in the period 1919 to 1923.
Before we can pass to an individual study of those countries
who have mainly influenced world events in our period we
must know something of these treaties.

On 11th November 1918 fighting on the western front ended
and the First World War was over. The 'central' powers of
Germany, Austria-Hungary, Turkey and Bulgaria had been
defeated by the Allies, although not without a terrible destruction and loss of life that had exhausted all the active
participants in the war. The appalling destruction of property in the battle areas was impossible to assess accurately.
Millions of lives were lost in the war, the British Commonwealth suffering over a million, Germany 2,300,000, France
1,300,000 and Russia over four million. The war had brought
about the downfall of four great empires—the German Hohenzollern, the Austro-Hungarian Habsburg, the Turkish Ottoman and the Russian Romanov. The immediate problem of
the victors—Britain, America, France, Italy and Japan being
the principal Allies—was a settlement with the defeated.
Russia had entered the war in 1914 as an Ally but in 1917
revolution had crippled her and she was soon out of the war.
By 1918 Russia was under the control of the Bolsheviks, to
whom the Allies were hostile, and she was not invited to take
part in the various peace treaties.

The peace settlement between victors and vanquished took
four years to complete, a separate treaty being signed

with each of the defeated countries. These treaties were as follows:

Date Signed	Name and Place of Treaty	Defeated Country Concerned
28th June 1919	Versailles	Germany
10th September 1919	St Germain	Austria
27th November 1919	Neuilly	Bulgaria
4th June 1920	Trianon	Hungary
23rd July 1923	Lausanne	Turkey

We will now consider these treaties in turn and try to arrive at some general conclusion concerning them.

TREATY OF VERSAILLES

Although they might dispute over various territorial claims, Lloyd George, Wilson, Clemenceau and Orlando—the chief representatives of the Allies—were definitely agreed on one thing at Versailles—Germany had been responsible for the war and she must be made to pay for her guilt in no uncertain way. Germany, who had been feared for many years, was broken and she must be made to realize war does not pay. The Versailles Treaty was, therefore, framed to give territorial rewards to those countries who had suffered German attack, and to weaken Germany in various ways so that she could not be a menace to peace again.

The territorial gains of the allies at the expense of Germany were based on President Wilson's principle of the return to their homelands of 'non-German' territory. Alsace-Lorraine, taken by Germany in the Franco-Prussian War of 1870, was returned to France. Eupen and Malmedy were acquired by Belgium. The new states of Czechoslovakia and Poland received, respectively, the Sudetenland (a predominantly German-speaking area) and the Posen territory. Various plebiscites were also held to decide the future of doubtful districts,

Treaty of Versailles

and in the plebiscites Germany lost further territory including north Schleswig to Denmark. The important pre-war ports of Memel and Danzig were made free cities under allied control. The valuable coal-mining area of the Saar was placed under French control for a period of fifteen years. At the end of this period a plebiscite was to be held to decide the Saar's future between France and Germany. It was also laid down in the Versailles Treaty that Germany's ally Austria must not amalgamate with Germany except with the permission of the Allies. By this territorial redistribution Germany lost over 25,000 square miles and seven million inhabitants of the former Hohenzollern Empire. To make Germany pay for the war damage she had caused, reparations to the Allies totalling £8,000,000,000 were charged to her, although many economists argued that the figure was unrealistic and would never be collected. They were to be proved right.

The military provisions of the Treaty allowed Germany an army not exceeding 100,000 men, and also drastically limited her ability to build up naval and air forces. Germany was not to indulge in any system of conscription.

MANDATES

Not only did Germany lose a good deal of territory in Europe but she also lost the whole of her colonial territory. Germany's overseas possessions had been occupied by the Allies during the war, and it was decided at Versailles that none of them would be returned to her. Most of these territories were divided between the Allies under the description of 'mandates'. The idea of a mandate was that the occupying power had a special duty towards the people of the territory and that every effort must be made to help them to eventually attain a level of development satisfactory for self-government. The former German colony of Tanganyika was divided as mandated territory between Britain, Belgium and Portugal. The Cameroons and Togoland were divided between Britain and France. South

The Peace Settlement 1919–1923

Africa was given responsibility for South West Africa. Germany's various Pacific possessions were placed under the control of Australia, New Zealand and Japan, the largest of them, German New Guinea, coming under Australian jurisdiction.

TREATY OF ST GERMAIN

One of the things you notice at once if you compare political maps of Europe before and after the First World War is the great increase in the number of sovereign states. If we include Turkey, from twenty-two sovereign states in Europe on the outbreak of the war, by 1919 twenty-eight had appeared and pre-war Serbia had expanded into the new state of Yugoslavia. These new countries emerged because of the break-up of the powerful pre-war German, Austro-Hungarian and Russian empires. Four of these new countries, Poland, Czechoslovakia, Hungary and Yugoslavia, owed their existence to the collapse of the Austro-Hungarian empire. The end of this anachronistic collection of different nations under the control of Austria was confirmed in the Treaty of St Germain.

From being the centre of a vast empire and regarded as one of the five great powers of Europe, Austria became by the Treaty a small country of seven million inhabitants, of whom two million lived in the capital Vienna. Hungary had become a separate state and by the Treaty the losses of territory to the new Poland and Yugoslavia were confirmed. The former provinces of Bohemia, Moravia and Slovakia were joined to become the new state of Czechoslovakia, and the South Tyrol was given to Italy as a reward for her destruction of the Austrian armies on the southern front. Austria's military forces were limited by the Treaty and she was also given an indemnity to pay.

Many Austrians in 1919, because of Austria's grave economic difficulties, would probably have preferred to join with Germany, but this was expressly forbidden by the Versailles Treaty.

Treaty of Neuilly

In terms of territorial losses Bulgaria suffered least of the defeated central powers. Her losses, in fact, as laid down in the Treaty of Neuilly, were little more than confirmations of the losses of previous wars. Greece received Bulgaria's Aegean coastline and Rumania the Dobrudja.

The clause of the Treaty which was to cause most bitterness to Bulgaria was the one guaranteeing her, 'economic outlets to the Aegean Sea'. Bulgaria took this at first to mean an actual corridor of territory similar to that given to Poland to link her with the Baltic. This clause finally, however, was only interpreted to give Bulgaria special privileges in some Greek port.

TREATY OF TRIANON

Hungary had become separated from Austria on the collapse of the central powers and a separate peace treaty was signed with her—the Treaty of Trianon. Although Austria had lost much territory formerly under her control by the Treaty of St Germain, nearly all this territory was inhabited by non-Austrians. The Treaty of Trianon, however, took from Hungary much territory where the overwhelming majority of the people were Magyars. Territory was lost to Czechoslovakia, Poland, Yugoslavia and a large area called Transylvania to Rumania. The Treaty of Trianon was received with much bitterness in Hungary.

TREATY OF LAUSANNE

The Treaty of Lausanne, signed by the Allies with Turkey in 1923, can be described as the most successful of all the peace treaties concluded at the end of the First World War. The Treaty was accepted as valid and applicable by its signatories for thirteen years, and even as late as 1936 was only modified by voluntary and general agreement. What reasons can we give for the success of this Treaty compared with the others? One reason was probably the fact that it was the last of the

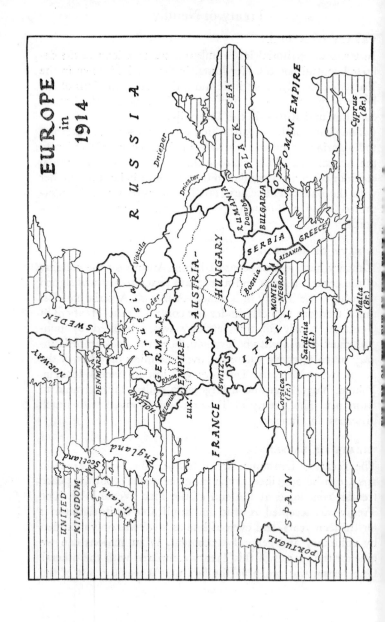

EUROPE
in
1914

THE EUROPE OF THE PEACE SETTLEMENT

peace treaties to be signed and by 1923 some of the hatred of the immediate post-war period may have abated. Secondly, the Treaty was negotiated and was not a purely imposed one as the others were. The Treaty, thirdly, was also discussed and signed on neutral soil, in Switzerland, and this may have been conducive to a better atmosphere in the talks.

The Treaty of Lausanne laid down that Turkey would relinquish all claims to the territory of the former Ottoman empire—Syria, Palestine, Iraq, Arabia and Jordan. The idea of mandates was applied to the former Turkish possessions of Syria, Palestine and Jordan. The responsibility for Syrian development was given to France, and Palestine and Jordan were placed under British control. Turkey would also pay a small indemnity and military restrictions had to be complied with. Although the territory lost by Turkey at Lausanne was greater than that of any other defeated central power it was still much less than what was at first demanded by the Allies. In August 1920 the Allies signed the notorious Treaty of Sèvres with the Turkish Sultan. This treaty reduced Turkey to Constantinople and north Anatolia, and Greece was given a large slice of the Anatolian hinterland. In 1920 Greek troops landed in Turkey to make good the Greek gains.

Many Turks were incensed by the harshness of the Treaty of Sèvres and led by a Turkish soldier called Kemal they declined to accept the authority of the Sultan (in Constantinople under allied occupation), established a new capital at Ankara in the interior, and, in 1922, defeated the Greeks and drove them from Anatolia.

The Allies at first considered taking up arms against Kemal and forcing Turkey to accept the Treaty of Sèvres, but finally good sense prevailed and allied and Turkish representatives met at Lausanne and drew up a treaty more acceptable to the Turks.

Kemal on achieving power abolished the Sultanate and

began the modernization of Turkey. Today he is regarded as the founder of the modern Turkish Republic.

GENERAL CONCLUSION

After summarizing the main provisions of the various peace treaties signed with the defeated central powers we can now try to arrive at some general conclusion concerning them.

It was true that the defeated countries bore the bulk of the guilt for the immense suffering and destruction of the First World War, and they deserved some retribution. It was just, too, that they should pay some compensation to their victims and opponents. It was also desirable to ensure that the defeated could not menace the peace of the world again. The end of the war also gave an opportunity to reform politically the map of the world in the light of the national aspirations of people. How far were these ideals attained in the treaties?

The military provisions of the treaties did seem to lay down that the defeated powers would be in no position in the future to repeat their aggressions, and all the treaties included compensation clauses. The creation of a number of new states, such as Poland and Czechoslovakia, also satisfied the desires of many national groups for their own governments. Except for that of Lausanne with Turkey, however, the treaties eventually failed to ensure peace. They were imposed on the defeated countries in an atmosphere of hatred and bitterness and contained the seeds of much future trouble. To reward countries who had suffered attack by the central powers many territories were transferred without any reference to the wishes of the population, although in some disputed areas plebiscites were held. Careful provision was also neglected for ensuring that the military provisions of the treaties could not be circumvented, and the amounts of compensation demanded from the defeated countries were on the whole unrealistic and could only lead to bankruptcy in the countries concerned.

The Peace Settlement 1919–1923

The allied statesmen at the treaty talks, however, genuinely believed that the peace settlement would last and that the 1914-1918 war was a war to end wars. But no attempt had been made to establish better relations with the defeated countries or to ensure that they would not fall under the control of elements who would exploit the bitterness left by the treaties. The seeds of the 1939-1945 war were already being sown in the settlement that brought to an end the war of 1914-1918.

FAR EAST

In November 1921 occurred the Washington Conference between the major powers interested in Far East affairs. The countries represented at the Conference were America, Britain, Japan, China, France, Holland, Portugal and two countries with no actual possessions in the Pacific area, Italy and Belgium. The various treaties described above did not touch on Far East affairs to any great extent (except to divide up the few Pacific colonies of Germany), and the Washington Conference met specifically to consider this important area. The rise of Japanese power in the Far East and her territorial ambitions had, by the beginning of the 'twenties, begun to cause acute concern to America and other western powers. America hoped at the Washington Conference to place limits on Japanese power and obtain some guarantee from her.

The result of the Conference appeared to be very satisfactory to the western participants. A four-power treaty was signed by America, Britain, France and Japan in which each agreed to respect each other's possessions in the Far East and abide by the *status quo*. The territorial integrity of China was also guaranteed by the Treaty. It was known that Japan had long been coveting Chinese territory in Manchuria. Japan also agreed to limit the number of capital ships in her navy to sixty per cent. of the number of capital ships in the British and American navies.

Far East

Although Japan at the Conference seemed to have satisfied the various demands of the western powers, she was soon to show that her desire for expansion gave no lasting value to the agreement.

LEAGUE OF NATIONS

At the end of the First World War hopes for peace and international co-operation were high amongst allied statesmen. This optimism is common to the immediate period following nearly all big wars. The war was described in newspapers as 'the war to end wars', and the general public in the victorious countries believed a happy era of peace was now at hand. The organization on which most of these hopes rested was the new international organization called the League of Nations. The idea of a world organization for peace and co-operation was not new. In the years before the first war enthusiastic internationalists such as Lord Robert Cecil in Britain and General Smuts in South Africa had campaigned for some international organization where the differences between states could be settled peacefully.

Towards the end of the First World War the idea of an international organization to ensure peace in the post-war period was again discussed by allied leaders, its most enthusiastic supporter being President Wilson of America. During the last few months of fighting in 1918 Wilson worked out in detail a constitution for this new world organization, and his proposed method of organizing the League was eventually accepted by Lloyd George and Clemenceau, the British and French premiers. The Covenant of the League, laying down its constitution and objectives, was incorporated into the Versailles Treaty.

As soon as the war ended a start was made in the formation of the new organization to be called the League of Nations. The main objective of the League was to provide a means of states discussing their problems and differences peacefully and so avoid wars. The League also aimed at jointly tackling the various outstanding problems of world reconstruction. It was decided that the League's meeting-place should be Geneva in Switzerland. All the allied countries, with the important exception of America, became members from the start. Britain also felt that the defeated countries should be allowed to become members also, but France would not allow this.

The machinery of the League was to consist of three main organs—a Council, an Assembly, and a Secretariat. The Council of the League was designed to give a weighting to the influence of the great powers and originally was to consist of five permanent members, Britain, America (who finally never joined the League), France, Italy and Japan, along with four non-permanent members elected by the Assembly for a short period. The Council was to meet at least three times a year. The Assembly of the League consisted of all the League members with equal voting power and was to meet at least once a year. The Secretariat of the League was its permanent administrative staff, or civil service as we might call it.

The League of Nations is now thought of as having been an abject failure. It is true that it did much good work in helping to suppress various social evils such as the drug traffic. It also successfully mediated in many territorial disputes between minor powers, such as Greece and Bulgaria, where otherwise prolonged fighting might have occurred. The League, however, failed finally to maintain peace, and by the thirties the high hopes of its founders were disappointed.

The League proved to be a failure for a number of reasons. In the first place, although it called itself League of Nations, it was never a universal organization. For reasons which we will go into in Chapter III America never joined the League, although President Wilson had been its main architect. The defeated central powers were also not allowed to join at first and Russia, under Bolshevik control when the League was formed and unpopular with the Allies, was also not invited.

League of Nations

In 1926 Germany was brought into the League but Hitler withdrew in 1934, the year that Russia finally gained admission. Japan left the League in 1933 after criticisms of her aggressions in China. Secondly, the League failed because its formation was linked from the start in the minds of the defeated countries with the maintenance of the peace treaties. The covenant of the League had been incorporated into the Versailles Treaty, and this, along with the refusal of France to allow German membership on the League's formation, led to Germany seeing little hope of the League being a means of revising the harsher aspects of the Versailles Treaty. Thirdly, we may say the League eventually failed because it lacked some coercive power to make its decisions binding on all—there was no powerful means at its disposal by which recalcitrant states could be brought to heel. Economic sanctions—depriving a country of certain vital raw materials—were tried against some aggressors but never with enough thoroughness to be really effective. The League was also formed in an atmosphere of great optimism by the democracies who saw the 1914–1918 war as a victory for democratic ideals over totalitarianism. The League would be an organization of democracies and these would surely be able to co-operate. Unfortunately, however, totalitarian ideas were far from dead and the spread of aggressive dictatorships in the inter-war period made peaceful international co-operation increasingly difficult. Finally, we must put down as one of the biggest factors in the League's final failure the problem of national sovereignty. The League always lacked real authority because the majority of states were not willing to give to it enough jurisdiction over their affairs to make it a really effective body.

We have already noted that Russia, one of the main Allies on the outbreak of war in 1914, did not take part in the peace settlement. We shall now turn to a consideration of Russia as the first of our individual studies of those major countries who have played significant roles in world affairs since 1919.

The Peace Settlement 1919–1923

READING LIST

The Lost Peace, H. Butler (Faber).

The League Experiment, E. E. Reynolds (Nelson).

International Relations between The Two World Wars 1919–1939, E. H. Carr (Macmillan).

Chapter Two

RUSSIA

The main problem of foreign affairs to our western democracies since the end of the Second World War in 1945 has been that of relations with Russia. In Britain in 1945 there was a great deal of good feeling towards Russia and admiration for her contribution to victory over the axis countries. In the three years which followed, however, this good feeling speedily gave way to a deep suspicion of Russia's intentions and a fear that she was bent on a policy of aggression. This fear, as we shall see in the last chapter of the book, led to the west rearming as a deterrent against the possibility of Russian aggression. A strengthening of our military position since 1948 has led us to hope that if Russia originally did have aggressive intentions towards us she may by now have realized our determination to defend our way of life and that some 'agreement to differ' may be possible with the Communist world. If we are to have good relations with Russia, or at least have some working agreement with her, then we must know more about the recent history of that country.

STATE OF RUSSIA IN 1914

Russia in 1914 was recognized as one of the great world powers. The Russian Empire stretched in the north from Finland to Alaska and in the south from Bessarabia to Vladivostok. This huge empire consisting of over a sixth of the land surface of the world, and containing many different races and religions, was ruled despotically from St Petersburg by Tsar Nicolas II and a small group of ministers appointed by him. In the first decade of the century there were attempts to introduce in the form of a Duma, or parliament, some limited form of representative government. By 1914, however, the power of this Duma had been crippled by the Tsar's retention of a right of veto over all legislation, and Russia was recognized as being, outside the Ottoman Empire, the most complete autocracy in Europe. The government did its utmost to stifle opposition: newspapers and all literature were censored; a secret police, the Okrana, kept a close watch on opponents of the régime, and exiled in Siberia were thousands of members of banned revolutionary movements such as the Bolshevik and Social Revolutionary parties. Over eighty per cent of the population were peasants and, despite the freeing of the serfs in 1861 and their theoretical freedom to move to the towns or any part of the country they wished, most of the peasants were virtually tied to some great estate on which their families had worked for centuries. The Russian aristocracy were incredibly wealthy, and pleasure-loving, with no conception of the need for great changes in Russia and of the impending disaster that was to overtake them. Many of the great Russian aristocratic families, such as the Youssoupoffs, owned estates larger than some of the Balkan kingdoms. There was no system of compulsory education in Russia and literacy was confined to only about ten per cent of the people. For the size of its population Russia had one of the smallest professional classes and intelligentsia in Europe. It was amongst the intelligentsia, and a small group of western educated aristocrats, that liberal opposition to the Tsarist régime was found. These progressives wanted Russia to attain a democratic system on British lines and worked for a Duma with greatly enlarged powers. They were suspicious of the violence preached by extreme revolutionaries and wanted a careful and gradual transformation of Russian society. These liberals possessed much idealism but their main fault was going to be shown in the future as a failure to act decisively and realistically in a moment of great crisis.

Opponents of Tsarism, who advocated a radical transformation of the régime, found that they were only safe when holding their large meetings abroad. Even then, they faced arrest when returning to Russia and many preferred to remain exiles. In the 'nineties and early years of the century small colonies of these revolutionaries began to gather in a number of European cities, particularly in Geneva and London. They published their own journals to discuss their views, the best known being the popular journal *Iskra* and the more academic *Zarya*. What was to become the All-Russian Communist Party (Bolsheviks) was founded as the Russian Social Democratic Workers' Party by a tiny congress of nine men in 1898 at Minsk. In 1903 the party held an important congress in Brussels. At this meeting a majority ('Bolsheviki') led by Lenin captured the party machine. This majority group were thorough-going Marxists, despising their fellow opponents of Tsarism who thought change might come gradually by means of industrial pressure and who laid stress on the important position of the peasant in Russian life. After the 1903 congress those minority groups ('Mensheviki') in the revolutionary movement largely became a separate, less radical, party of their own.

THE RUSSIAN REVOLUTION OF MARCH 1917

Although we speak of the Russian Revolution of 1917 and often hardly think of any interval between the downfall of Tsarism and the seizure of power by the Bolsheviks, it is more accurate to speak in the plural of Russian Revolutions. The initial revolution which caused the Tsar's abdication brought to power not the Bolsheviks but those liberal elements we have spoken of above. We must now briefly summarize the reasons for the downfall of the Romanov dynasty.

After some initial successes in 1914 when the war broke out, the Russian armies which had invaded Prussia were routed at Tannenburg and the Masurian Lakes. During the next three years the German armies advanced into the Ukraine, White Russia and along the Baltic seaboard. By the beginning of

1917 the Imperial Russian Army (once considered the most formidable army in Europe) because of bad leadership and lack of arms was at the end of its tether. Meanwhile, behind the front, hostility was growing towards the Imperial régime. It was rumoured that the Tsarina—who seemed fated to play the part of a Marie Antoinette—was in correspondence with the enemy, and was dominated by a debauched monk called Rasputin. Food was scarce in Russian cities and country areas were seriously affected by the loss of men to the army. Despite advice that he should immediately institute a series of liberal measures to gain popular support, the Tsar refused to relinquish any of his powers, and finally took the disastrous step of assuming supreme command of the defeated army. Military defeat and growing dissatisfaction at home, coupled with the Tsar's refusal to grant concessions, finally brought the country to the point of revolution.

At the beginning of March 1917 many of the factory workers in St Petersburg were on strike. On March 10th these strikers staged demonstrations in the capital and were joined by the city's students and by many sympathisers. Cossack detachments, previously always very reliable defenders of the autocracy, also openly fraternized with the demonstrators. By the next day, March 11th, the situation appeared to the authorities to be getting out of hand and the police and city's military cadets were ordered to quell the revolt. During the day the police and cadets shot down over 150 of the strikers but even this did not clear the streets and when on the next day, March 12th, the Preobrazkenski Regiment—the main regiment garrisoning the capital—joined the crowds, it was obvious that a revolution was in progress. Even at this late stage, however, Nicolas II refused to believe that the situation was desperate and ordered the now helpless governor of St Petersburg to clear the streets and restore order. The capital by now, however, was in the hands of the mob and on March 14th the Tsar abdicated and requested that he and his family be allowed to leave for Britain.

The Russian Revolution of March 1917

After the Tsar's abdication it appeared for a few days as if some form of limited monarchy under the Tsar's brother might emerge, but eventually the new Provisional Government which had been formed declared the creation of a Russian Republic. This new Provisional Government was headed by two moderate politicians called Prince Lvov, a liberal, and Kerensky, a democratic socialist. This new government gave itself two main tasks: firstly, the granting to Russia of a new democratic system of government that would make it more like a western country such as Britain or France, and the continuance of the war against the Central Powers until an allied victory had been won. Although the new régime was welcomed at first in Russia by all those moderate elements who had opposed Tsarism, and Kerensky appeared to be very popular, it soon became obvious in the weeks following the March Revolution that real political power lay in the hands of the Bolsheviks, so we must now turn our attention to them.

SEIZURE OF POWER BY THE BOLSHEVIKS, NOVEMBER 1917

Immediately on taking power the Provisional Government declared freedom of religion, political association and of the press throughout Russia, and released the many thousands of Tsarist political prisoners held in Siberia. These opponents of the old Tsarist régime, many of them extreme revolutionaries, flooded back into St Petersburg and European Russia. Among them was a Bolshevik Communist revolutionary called Djugashvili whom we shall hear much of later under the name of Stalin. When the March Revolution occurred, the Germans welcomed it as an event which would further weaken Russia and help them to put her completely out of the war. With Russia out of the war, the German High Command reasoned, the German troops on the eastern front could be concentrated for a knockout blow in the west before the new American armies could make themselves felt. To sow dissension in Russia, therefore, the Germans allowed a well-known Bolshevik, Lenin, to make his way through the front line and back into Russia.

Russia

Another Communist leader, Trotsky, also returned to Russia and these Communist leaders began to organize themselves in St Petersburg (now rechristened Petrograd by the Provisional Government) to seize power from the Provisional Government.

Although the Provisional Government was at first very popular, support for it gradually weakened during the weeks following the March Revolution. Kerensky had ordered a disastrous offensive against the enemy and the continued prosecution of the war became increasingly unpopular. Great measures of industrial and land reform were necessary if the new government was to remain in power, but the Provisional Government during its first three months of office showed little sign that it was prepared to act quickly to implement its promises on these questions. In this situation of a vacillating government, an unpopular war, and increasing lawlessness in country areas the Communist Party saw its opportunity to seize power and began to organize soviets i.e. local councils of workers, soldiers and peasants in St Petersburg and throughout Russia.

On November 7th, 1917, a second revolution staged by the Communists occurred in St Petersburg and the short-lived Provisional Government was overthrown. Kerensky thought at first of marching on the capital with troops from the front and arresting the Communist leaders, but when he realized that control of the army had also passed to the soviets he fled to Finland. Lenin became the head of a new Communist government and Russia was declared a Union of Soviet Socialist Republics. Russia, Lenin declared, was to be transformed into a socialist society under the leadership of the Russian Communist Party.

The new Communist government faced many problems; but before describing these problems we must spend some time discussing the political theory on which their approach to government was based. In Russia today all aspects of life—politics, economics, foreign affairs, the arts, sport and everything else—are finally regarded in terms of a theory we call

Seizure of Power by the Bolsheviks, November 1917

Marxism. It is true that, although the Communists in power in Russia since 1917 have accounted for all their policies in terms of Marxism, in many cases their actions have been dictated by other factors, such as expediency and a love of power, and only explained afterwards by references to Marxism. Many of their policies, however, have stemmed from the Marxist theory they subscribe to, and we shall not be able to understand the history of the Soviet Union unless we know something about this theory.

COMMUNIST THEORY

The theory we know as Marxism is derived from the writings of two ninetcenth-century thinkers, Karl Marx (1818–1883) and Frederick Engels (1820–1895). The principal books written by Marx were *The Poverty of Philosophy* (1847), *Critique of Political Economy* (1859) and *Capital* (1867). Engels wrote *The Condition of the Working Class in England in 1844* (1844), and both writers collaborated in writing the small, but explosive in its effects, *The Communist Manifesto* (1848). It is in *The Communist Manifesto* that we can find a concise statement of the communist position and we shall now summarize its arguments.

Marx and Engels were interested in attempting to study history in what they considered to be a scientific way. They wanted to show that social change had a pattern to it and in *The Communist Manifesto* set down their view that the root of all social change lies in one main factor, the economic—the way men produce things to satisfy their material needs. The way men live and are ruled in society now, and the way societies have been organized in the past, Marx and Engels wrote, rest on the economic factor of the way wealth is produced.

Political power rests with those who own the means of producing wealth, and so in nineteenth-century industrialized Europe the control of states rested with the factory owners. In fact, wrote Marx and Engels, we now have two classes, the bourgeoisie—those who own the means of production—and

39

the proletariat—those who have no means of earning a living except by selling their labour—and today,

'the executive of the modern state is but a committee for managing the common affairs of the whole bourgeoisie.'[1]

Historical development, however, follows a pattern and capitalist or bourgeois society will inevitably give way to a different form of society organized for the benefit of the proletariat. Capitalism is doomed,

'Its fall and the victory of the proletariat are equally inevitable.'[2]

The job of the Communist Party, the *élite* and leaders of the proletariat, is to seize power when the moment is ripe and build a socialist society where economic life is controlled by the state. This socialist stage is described as the dictatorship of the proletariat and during this stage the Communist leaders will have to defeat any counter-revolution from the bourgeoisie and bring about enormous social changes. As capitalism eventually disintegrates over the whole of the world a world socialist society will appear. This socialist society will in turn give way to an ideal Communist society where the state has withered away and there is no need for a central coercive authority. A summary of the Marxist theory of history is then, as follows:—

1. History can be studied scientifically.
2. After studying history one fundamental factor governing all social change can be found—the economic factor.
3. The way of life in any society stems from the ways in which production is organized and control of the state lies with those who control the means of production.
4. Two classes now exist—the bourgeoisie, who control the state, and the proletariat, who live by selling their labour.
5. This form of society will inevitably give way to a socialist form of society controlled by the Communist Party.

[1], [2] Marx and Engels: *The Communist Manifesto*. Part I (1848).

Communist Theory

6. The Communist Party is to seize power when the opportunity presents itself and to control the economic life of the state in the interests of the proletariat. It is to destroy bourgeois attempts to overthrow them.

7. Eventually capitalism will decay everywhere and a world socialism will lead to the ideal Communist society where there will be no need for governments.

CRITICISM OF COMMUNIST THEORY

Our criticism of the above theory can be on a number of grounds. The first point about the theory which makes it unsatisfactory is its monist—one factor—nature. A careful objective approach to the study of society is necessary if we are to build up a body of accurate data about social relations. This approach, however, leads us to grasp the complexity of social life and the fact that many different factors underlie the form of society we live in. Marxist theory lays down that there is only one basic factor governing social form and change, and while we can agree in the importance of the economic factor in life, we cannot agree that there are no other factors of equal importance. A variety of other criticisms of the theory suggest themselves to us—why, for instance, if capitalist society is doomed anyway should Communists go to such trouble in working for the overthrow of capitalism? The Marxist would reply here, of course, that it is the job of the Communist Party to hasten the historical process, but there still seems to be in Marxist writing an unhappy relationship between a determinist theory and calls for support for the Communist Party. Marxist theory also over simplifies in its definition of two classes in capitalist society, and its view that a dictatorship of the Communist Party would at some stage be voluntarily relinquished by the dictators seems unreal in the light of history.

For all its inadequacies Marxist doctrine has been a formidable challenge to democracy since the end of the war in 1945. Its attractiveness has lain to the thinker in its simplicity and to the under-privileged in its claim that the rule of the Communist Party would provide a higher standard of life. Later in this book we shall show that democracy can meet the challenge of Communism. Despite its unsatisfactory nature, however, Marxism was the theory which Bolshevik leaders, who had come to power by the November Revolution, were to use to explain their policies, in fact, many of their policies were to be the direct result of their subscribing to the theory.

STATE OF RUSSIA IN 1919

We have already noted that Russia was not a signatory to the various treaties which followed the ending of the First World War in 1918. Russia had entered the war in 1914 as an ally of Britain and France against the Central Powers and expected at the end of the war to receive substantial territorial gains as a prize. When the Bolsheviks seized power in November 1917 they immediately entered into talks with the Germans to bring the war on the eastern front to an end. The Bolsheviks described the war as an 'imperialist' one which they did not believe in, and they wished to end what was now a hopeless conflict for Russia's demoralized armies. In December 1917 the new Bolshevik government signed with the Germans the Treaty of Brest-Litovsk ceding to Germany the Baltic coastline, Finland and the Ukraine. This defection of Russia and the revolutionary nature of her new régime led to western hostility, and Britain and France began to hope that the Bolsheviks would be overthrown. By 1919 Russia was surrounded by a hostile world.

Meanwhile the situation in Russia in 1919 appeared chaotic. Large areas of the country had been ravaged by war, and epidemics and famine were rife. Orderly government hardly existed outside the main cities and not only did the Bolsheviks have hostile foreign powers to combat but also those elements inside Russia who were determined to overthrow the November Revolution. After the Bolsheviks came to power various so-called 'white' armies under the leadership of former officers of the Tsarist army appeared in Russia to suppress the Revolution. The whole of Siberia fell under the control of Admiral Kolchak, who was recognized by the allied powers as 'Regent of all the Russias'; the Baltic states were occupied by anti-Bolshevik forces under General Yudenitch; Archangel and the north by General Miller's army, and the Crimea and south by General Deniken's forces. British troops entered the oil areas of the Caucasus and French troops occupied Odessa. Although by 1919 most of these white armies had been destroyed by a hastily improvised red army, and foreign troops withdrawn, the Crimea was still under the control of General Wrangel's anti-Bolshevik army.

PROBLEMS FACING THE COMMUNISTS

The following tasks had to be tackled in 1919 by Lenin's government:

1. The defeat of the remaining white armies and the destruction of so-called bourgeois counter-revolutionary elements.
2. The securing of effective control over the whole of Russia to usher in the dictatorship of the proletariat.
3. The state control of Russian economic life and the building up of backward Russia as an industrial country.
4. The education of the backward masses of Russia in order to provide the type of population needed by a modern country.

The immediate problems, however, were the defeat of Wrangel and the restoring of orderly government throughout Russia. In 1920 the red army stormed the Perekop Isthmus leading into the Crimea and the last white army was defeated. By the end of the same year the Communist government in Moscow (Lenin had moved the capital from Petrograd to Moscow) could feel itself master of the whole country.

Before going on to describe how Russia was built up into the great industrial and world power she is today, let us look at

Russia

the stories of some of the Communist leaders who in 1919 found themselves the dictators of the biggest country in the world.

THE BOLSHEVIK LEADERS

The most important of the Bolshevik leaders were Lenin, Trotsky and Stalin.

Lenin (1870–1924): Vladimir Ilych Ulyanov, known as Lenin, was born into a prosperous professional family living in Simbirsk, now called Ulyanovsk after the name of his family. It is interesting that Lenin was a revolutionary before he came into contact with Marxist writing. Two events in his early life were to have a great effect on him and to make him a convinced opponent of Tsarism. The first event was his banishment to the country in 1887 from Kazan University where he had taken part in a revolutionary meeting. The second event was the execution in 1891 of his eldest brother for taking part in an unsuccessful plot against the life of Tsar Alexander III. After returning to Kazan in 1889 he began a systematic study of Marxism and felt it provided the theoretical basis for his revolutionary activities. In 1894 he moved to St Petersburg and organized the illegal 'Union for the Liberation of the Working Class'. In 1895 Lenin was arrested and spent over three years in Siberia. During this period he wrote his most important economic work *The Development of Capitalism in Russia*. In 1900 on returning from Siberia he left Russia and went to live in Switzerland. It was in Switzerland that Lenin and his Marxist supporters (Bolsheviks) broke with the moderate reformers (Mensheviks). On the outbreak of war in 1914 Lenin denounced all those socialists who supported their governments. To Lenin the war was an 'Imperialist' one which the working class should use for the overthrow of capitalism. After the abdication of the Tsar in February 1917 Lenin returned to Russia and spent the next eight months organizing the soviets. In November 1917 he overthrew the Provisional Government of Kerensky and declared the dictatorship of the proletariat. During the remaining

44

The Bolshevik Leaders

seven years of his life Lenin worked for the creation in Russia of the socialist society which his Marxism taught was the first step to the ideal Communist society. In attempting to found this society he showed a greater realism and humanity than many of his followers, but finally his decisions were dictated by a clear political goal. Professor Carr has written of Lenin:

'It has become a commonplace to praise Lenin's realism, his flexibility, his practical common sense in judging what could and what could not be done at the given moment; and all these qualities he possessed in pre-eminent degree. But perhaps the most vivid impression left by a re-reading of his major works is of the amazing intellectual power and consistency of purpose which runs through them. His tactical readiness to compromise, to tack, to retreat when it became necessary was an enormous asset to a politician. But what is infinitely more striking is that he seems to have known from the first where he was going and how he intended to get there, and that when he died in 1924 the revolution was firmly established on foundations which he had begun to dig thirty years before'.[1]

In August 1918 a political opponent of Lenin called Kaplan fired two shots and wounded him when he was on his way to a meeting in St Petersburg. This wound, the effects of his past imprisonments and overwork all sapped his strength and he died on January 21st, 1924, near Moscow. Although he considered only the bases had been laid of the socialist society he wished to build Lenin could feel before his death, that his party were now firmly in control. Great honours were accorded Lenin on his death and the old capital of St Petersburg (rechristened Petrograd by Kerensky's Government) was given the new name of Leningrad.

Trotsky (1879–1940): Leo Davidovitch Bronstein, better known as Trotsky, was born of a Jewish commercial family in

[1] E. H. Carr. *Studies in Revolution*, Chapter IX. Lenin: The Master Builder. Macmillan, 1950.

Elizavetgrad. He was educated at Odessa University and arrested for revolutionary activities when only nineteen and exiled to Siberia. In 1902 he escaped to England by using the false name of Trotsky and afterwards assumed this name permanently. It was in London that he met Lenin and soon became a convinced Marxist, although at first attempting an independent position between the Bolsheviks and Mensheviks. During his exile from Russia he travelled widely and visited England, France, Switzerland, Turkey and was in America in 1916 as editor of the Russian revolutionary journal *Novy Mir*. When the February Revolution broke out the subscribers to *Novy Mir* collected enough money for his return to Russia. Although he did not actually join the Bolsheviks until July 1917 he played an important part in the overthrow of the Provisional Government in November of that year. Trotsky became foreign minister under Lenin and signed the notorious Treaty of Brest-Litovsk with Germany. The defeat of the white armies was mainly because of Trotsky's hard work in raising an efficient red army out of the demoralized Russian troops of 1917. Under his leadership this red army proved itself, although poorly equipped, to be a fighting force of high morale. Trotsky showed his military sense when he advised against the red army advancing on Warsaw in 1920. This advance took place and the red army was decisively beaten by Polish troops. On the death of Lenin in 1924 many foreign observers expected that Trotsky would automatically fill Lenin's place as head of state. Trotsky became involved in 1924, however, with a struggle for power with Stalin and was out-manœuvred by Stalin in 1927. In 1929 he was banished from Russia and eventually went to live in Mexico. Trotsky still had many supporters—Trotskyists—throughout the world and these believed in his idea of a world revolution rather than Russian Communists attempting to build socialism merely in their own country. In 1940 Trotsky was murdered, and it is possible that his death was plotted by Stalin.

Stalin (1879–1953): Joseph Vissarionovitch Djugashvili,

better known by his name of Stalin, the man of steel, was born the son of a poor Georgian shoemaking family. His mother, a deeply religious woman, wanted Joseph to study for the priesthood of the Greek Orthodox Church, and he was selected for a course at a Russian religious seminary. By the age of sixteen, however, Stalin had become a speaker in the seminary against Tsarism and he was expelled. At seventeen he had already become a prominent member of a Georgian revolutionary group and to obtain funds for this organization carried out a number of daring bank robberies. Between 1902 and 1912 he was arrested four times but each time managed to escape. In 1913 he was exiled to Siberia and did not return to St Petersburg until the release of political prisoners by the Provisional Government in February 1917. After the Bolshevik seizure of power in November 1917 Stalin became a member of Lenin's government as commissar for minorities. This was not a very important post, but Stalin soon became prominent for his defence of Tsaritsyn, an important town on the Volga, against the attack of General Deniken's white army. Stalin also organized the defence of this town under its new name of Stalingrad against the German army of Von Paulus in the Second World War. From 1920 to 1923 Stalin was a member of the small inner cabinet of Bolsheviks under Lenin who controlled Russia. Lenin, with whom Stalin tried repeatedly to ingratiate himself, remained suspicious of his lieutenant to the end and suspected that Stalin might want to play the part of Napoleon. On Lenin's death in 1924 it was thought that Trotsky would succeed him as the new Bolshevik leader. Stalin had, however, by 1924 become General Secretary of the Russian Communist Party and used this powerful post to begin a struggle for power with Trotsky. With the exiling of Trotsky in 1929 Stalin emerged as the new strong man of Russia. In the decade before the outbreak of war in 1939 Stalin built himself up into more of a despotic position than that enjoyed by any of the Tsars. Many of the other 'old Bolsheviks' who had taken part in the November Revolution were eliminated in this period by various purge trials. During the war against Germany Stalin built up a reputation for himself as a great war leader but his powers of generalship were probably much exaggerated. Stalin represented Russia at the various war-time conferences with Britain and America and extracted the maximum concessions for Russia in the conferences. After the end of the war there were constant reports in the west that Stalin was seriously ill and these reports caused much conjecture as to what would happen in Russia in the event of his death. In March 1953 Stalin died of a heart attack and was succeeded by Malenkov. It was hoped in the west that this change of Russia's leadership would lead to a friendlier foreign policy by Russia.

SOCIALISM IN ONE COUNTRY

We have already seen how by 1920 Lenin and his party were in effective control in Russia. Foreign intervention had ended, the white armies had been destroyed, and an emigration of of several million 'white' Russians who feared the new régime meant that little internal opposition was to be expected. One great question now faced the Bolsheviks. Should they look upon the Russian Revolution as merely the first of a series of imminent Communist revolutions throughout the world and should they now concentrate on realizing world control and the building of a world socialist society? Or should they take the view that the collapse of capitalism abroad was not imminent and that the building, as Stalin put it, of 'Socialism in one country" must be first pursued? We have said something above about the struggle for power between Stalin and Trotsky on Lenin's death. This struggle was primarily one between personalities who wished to assume the supreme dictatorship left by Lenin. It assumed, however, the form of a struggle between the protagonists of world revolution and the supporters of socialism in one country. Deutscher has written of this struggle:

'The dilemma to which this gave rise was in the centre of the struggle between Stalin and Trotsky. To use terms now current, Bolsheviks had to decide whether it should go on staking its future on the "liberation", that is on the self-emancipation, of foreign working classes or whether it ought to aim at "containing" capitalism at the frontiers of the Soviet Union'.[1]

It was Trotsky who was the advocate of world revolution and Stalin who was the advocate of a policy of first concentrating on the building of socialism in Russia. With the exiling of Trotsky in 1929 the battle between the Trotskyists and Stalinists ended in Russia, but well before this year the idea of any imminent world overthrow of capitalism had lost ground among the Russian Communists.

RUSSIAN INDUSTRY SINCE 1919

The building of Russia into a socialist society with a rising standard of living necessitated a policy of rapid industrialization. The most outstanding aspect of the history of the Soviet Union has been its economic transformation from a backward country with few industrial centres into one of the leading industrial powers of the world. This transformation can be compared with the industrialization which transformed Britain in the nineteenth century into the workshop of the world. Whereas our industrialization, however, was the culmination of a process which had been going on for a century, Russia's transformation took place in the space of only thirty years and was the product of ruthless state planning.

Although Tsarist Russia had seen a good deal of economic progress at the end of the last century under the direction of a progressive minister called Count Witte, the country could still be described as being very backward industrially. Jorré has summarized Russia's economic position at this time as follows:

'A country thirty-eight times as big as France had hardly twice the length of railways. Above all, industrial production remained small. Russia had never been known to have

[1] Deutscher. *Russia after Stalin.* Chapter II. From Leninism to Stalinism. Hamilton, 1953.

such great relative advance as in the time of Witte, it is true; but in 1913 the empire was producing only twenty-nine million tons of coal a year (or 2.4 per cent of world production), five times less electric power than Germany, and seventeen times less than the United States. It had only four and a half million tons of cast iron and the same quantity of steel (five per cent of world production). Considering the greater progress of rivals, even of France, which was merely an average industrial power, Russian inferiority continued to increase in nearly every branch. "We are falling behind more and more" wrote Lenin.

There were worse things. Since the industry had been created by foreign capital, and was protected by tariffs, it was usually badly managed and equipped and produced only inferior goods. Though the workmen were paid very small wages production costs were very high and therefore the goods could find no market abroad. The only buyer was the State, which was both producer and consumer. Hence, industry was in a condition of latent crisis and was continually threatened with bankruptcy.'[1]

This was the economic system the Bolsheviks set out to revolutionize. The overall planning by the state of Russia's economic life did not really get under way until 1928. After some disastrous attempts at overall planning Lenin had instituted his New Economic Policy (known as NEP) which had allowed a good deal of private enterprise. In 1928 the Soviet Union embarked on its scheme of five-year plans, designed to give the country a modern industrial system,

'progress along these lines would permit of advance in other directions, which would be increasingly marked and rapid during the subsequent five-year periods. Soon the Soviet Union would "overtake and pass the capitalist countries", including the United States, whose economic greatness haunted the minds of the Russians. Then its military power

[1] G. Jorré. *The Soviet Union.* Part III, Chapter X. 'The Backward Economic System under the Tsars.' Longmans, Green, 1950.

would be such that it would no longer have anything to fear from any state or coalition. The considerable rise in the standard of living would indissolubly attach the masses to the Soviet system, and as the Union would beome a "social paradise" in the eyes of all the workers on the globe, its example would be the most effective propaganda to bring about the downfall of capitalism in the west.'[1]

This was the ideal aimed at by Stalin and underlying the five-year plans.

Under the control of Gosplan (State Planning Board) Soviet industry began to make rapid strides. This economic transformation of the country was only pushed through at the cost of rigid state planning of the lives of Russians, the elimination of those who proved awkward, and the utilization of large forced labour groups numbering millions of opponents of the régime. At a terrific price in human suffering, however, Soviet production rose steadily as the example given in the following tables show:—

BASIC INDUSTRIAL FIGURES FOR GERMANY (EXCLUDING TERRITORIES ANNEXED BY HITLER) AND RUSSIA IN 1929 AND 1940[2]

		1929	1940
OUTPUT OF COAL	Russia	41	166
(in millions of tons)	Germany	177	185–190
STEEL	Russia	5	18
(in millions of tons)	Germany	18	20
ELECTRICITY	Russia	6	48
(in billions of KWH)	Germany	30	55
GOODS TRAFFIC ON RAILWAYS	Russia	187	590
(in millions of tons)	Germany	463	500 (approx)

[1] G. Jorré. *The Soviet Union.* Part III, Chapter X. 'The Backward Economic System under the Tsars.' Longmans, Green, 1950.
[2] This table is taken from I. Deutscher. *Russia After Stalin.*

Russia

BASIC PRODUCTION[1]

MILLION METRIC TONS

	U.S.S.R. in 1951	U.K., France and West Germany 1951	U.S.A. 1951
COAL	281	398	523
OIL	42	1.7	309
ELECTRICITY (billion KWH)	103	147	370
PIG IRON	22	29	63
CRUDE STEEL	31	39	95

From being one of Europe's most backward countries economically in 1919 Russia has today one of the most powerful economic systems in the world. The devastation caused by the war with Germany 1941–1945 proved a serious setback to her economic development, but further rapid strides have been achieved since the end of the war. Deutscher writes:

'Whether or not Russia will ever be able to realize her ambition of attaining industrial parity with the United States, the mere fact that she is about to leave behind the combined industrial power of Western Europe and is thinking ahead so ambitiously, gives a measure of the profound transformation she has undergone in the Stalin era.'[2]

AGRICULTURE

Russia in 1919 was primarily an agricultural country and even today, after thirty years of industrialization, agriculture remains the chief occupation of the people. There have been very great agricultural changes in the Soviet Union. Contemporary with rapid industrialization there was a revolution in the tenure of land in Russia. By 1939 only a few privately

[1] This table is taken from I. Deutscher. *Russia After Stalin.*

[2] I. Deutscher. *Russia after Stalin.* Chapter Two. From Leninism to Stalinism.

Agriculture

owned farms remained, the rest having been taken over by the state and 'collectivized'.

The state control of agriculture in the Soviet Union takes two forms. Firstly, there are the *sovkhozes* which are huge farm communities usually concentrating on one product and treating the agricultural workers in them with a military discipline. The production of the *sovkhozes* has never been as high as originally desired but they have been retained because they provide what is considered to be a valuable training for their agricultural workers who will usually leave at some time to work in *kolkhozes*.

The *kolkhozes*, or collective farms, usually produce a variety of products and are not organized so much on the agricultural college lines of the *sovkhozes*. Although the bulk of the land and livestock in a *kolkhoze* is owned by the state a certain amount of private property is allowed. Work and machinery are shared and after deducting the needs of the workers in the *kolkhoze* the remaining products are sold to state organizations and prices fixed by the government.

Although the mechanization of agriculture and a greater use of scientific methods have considerably raised agricultural production in the Soviet Union it is only recently that any substantial body of agricultural workers in Russia have been won over to it. The Collectivization of agriculture when it was first put into operation resulted in some of the worst excesses of the Bolshevik régime, and in the extermination of the wealthier farmers—the *kulaks*—who opposed it and who were sent to forced labour camps.

STALIN CONSTITUTION OF 1936

The present Soviet system of government is based on the Constitution written in 1936 and named after Stalin, its principal author. Russia claims to be a federal country, like the United States of America, consisting of a number of states linked together. The 1936 Constitution provides for a two-chamber system of government. These two houses, the Council of the

Union and the Council of Nationalities, together form the Soviet Parliament or Supreme Soviet.

The Council of the Union is elected over the whole country by a system of proportional representation and is supposed mainly to consider national questions. The Council of Nationalities contains representatives from the various Soviet republics (the number from each state based on its status) and this body is supposed to represent the interests of the various republics in the central government. The Supreme Soviet according to the 1936 Constitution meets annually, but in practice the meetings have only occurred at long intervals (the first meeting since the outbreak of the Second World War was not held until 1953). The members of these two houses do not regard their position as anything approaching a full-time job and as we shall see in a moment their real powers are almost non-existent. The franchise, right to vote, in Russia is possessed by all adult men and women, except certain 'enemies of the state', and general elections are held for both houses of the Supreme Soviet.

The real law-making body in the Soviet system of government is the Presidium of the Supreme Soviet presided over by Stalin before his death. The Presidium today consists of thirty-three professional politicians who are almost permanently in session. These are the chief ministers of the Soviet Union. Most of the important laws passed in Russia since the end of the war have been announced by the Presidium without reference to the two houses of the Supreme Soviet, and changes in the constitution can be decreed by the Presidium without reference to the Supreme Soviet.

Each of the constituent republics also have their own governments, but the powers of these state governments are mainly restricted to certain cultural matters. For all its theoretical federal nature the Russian system of government is highly centralized.

Is the Soviet Union a democracy? Communists claim that she is and, in fact, claim that Russia is far more of a 'real democracy' than our western countries. What truth is there in this? Superficially the Soviet Constitution may appear democratic but on a number of fundamentals it cannot be described as a democracy as we understand it.

In western countries we understand democracy as resting on a party system offering a real choice of government to the electorate, and the executive, the body of ministers, being responsible in some way to the elected representatives or directly to the people.

These things, however, do not apply to the Russian system. Only candidates approved by the Communist Party are allowed to stand in elections and the group of ministers are also leading members of the Communist Party and not answerable to the Supreme Soviet. Russia is, then, a one-party state with an executive not removable by the legislature. It seems appropriate at this point to consider the position of the Communist Party in Russia.

THE COMMUNIST PARTY IN RUSSIA

Contrary to popular opinion not all Russians are members of the Communist Party. The Communist Party was described in *The Communist Manifesto* of 1848 as the élite of the working class, and as those who have the necessary knowledge of history and determination to lead the state on Marxist lines. The Russian Communist Party has always worked on this basis and has made membership a privilege and an honour. When the party first came to power in 1917 membership only numbered 25,000, and as late as 1940 when the population of Russia numbered 200,000,000 the Communist Party had only 2,500,000 full members. Because of a more liberal policy of admission during the war years the party now numbers 7,000,000 but this still represents only five per cent of the adult population.

Controlling the party is the Central Committe of the Communist Party whose nucleus of thirty-six form a policy-making Presidium. It is this group which frames the measures to be passed by the Presidium of the Supreme Council and, in fact, membership of the two Presidiums is usually almost identical.

SOVIET EDUCATION

When they came to power in 1917 the Communists realized that education was a vital weapon in their hands. Firstly, it was the means of producing a large number of technically qualified people necessary for the terrific expansion of Russia's industries which had been planned. But, secondly, and even more important than this to the Communists, education appeared as the means of creating a politically conscious people—to the Communist a population well grounded in Marxist theory. It was decided that backward Tsarist education had to be completely refashioned to meet these two needs. For the first decade they were in power all sorts of educational experiments were carried out by the Communists.

'Thus, for a number of years Soviet Russia became a huge educational laboratory. School discipline was thrown overboard, homework and examinations were abolished, and teachers were deprived of their authority. The schools were run by special school councils on which the pupils were represented. At the same time, the school curriculum underwent drastic and revolutionary changes; the main stress was put on technical subjects and on the A B C of Communism, the so-called "political grammar".'[1]

By the 'thirties a reaction to this experimental period set in and there was a return to rigid school discipline and to older educational methods. A large part of the curriculum, however, continued to be devoted to the teaching of Marxist theory and beginnings in this are made before Soviet children reach the 'teens. It is in the schools that future Soviet citizens are first acquainted with such terms as 'Fascist agents' and 'Trotskyists' and the rest of the vocabulary of Marxist abuse.

[1] W. Kolarz. *How Russia is Ruled.* Chapter IX. 'Communist Education.' The Batchworth Press, 1953.

Soviet Education

An important part of the educational system is considered by the Communists to be the Communist Youth Movement— the Young Pioneers. The Pioneers number today nearly 20,000,000 Russian children between the ages of nine and fifteen. After leaving the Pioneers a Russian teen-ager may join the Communist Youth League, or Komsomol as it is called. The majority of Komsomol meetings are devoted to an intensive study of Marxist texts. If selected as a potential Communist leader it is possible to graduate from the Komsomol as a probationary member of the Communist Party.

RELIGION IN SOVIET RUSSIA

Marx described religion as 'the opiate of the people', and the Bolsheviks when they first came to power regarded the Greek Orthodox Church—the main church in Russia—with open hostility. Religion, according to the Communists, was a bourgeois plot designed to focus the attention of the miserable proletariat on a mythical paradise to come and to make them forget their present injustices. The Communists considered the Greek Orthodox Church as well to have been one of the main bulwarks of Tsarism.

Because the majority of Russians were firm members of the Greek Church the Communists could not abolish it by one decree. They therefore decided in 1917 on a policy of placing many restrictions in the way of the priesthood so that there were few opportunities for practising religion. At the same time as this the Communists began to pursue a policy of anti-religious propaganda and education.

In 1925 a department of the Communist Party was founded called the League of Militant Godless, and this body under its chief Yaroslavsky carried out violent propaganda against religion between 1925 and 1941. In 1925 the Patriarch of Moscow—the head of the Greek Orthodox Church in Russia —died and the Communists did not allow the election of a successor.

When the war with Germany broke out in 1941 Stalin saw

in the Greek Church an opportunity of gaining further support for the régime. The Greek Orthodox Church was allowed to elect a new Patriarch and a greater degree of religious toleration was permitted. In return for these favours an unquestioned loyalty to the régime was demanded from the Church. Stalin also probably hoped that the revival of the post of Patriarch would be a further means of spreading Russian influence abroad among members of the Greek Orthodox Church.

SOVIET FOREIGN RELATIONS

At the end of 1918 the Soviet Union was surrounded by a hostile world. Foreign armies were on her soil and very active aid was being given to the anti-Bolshevik armies by foreign governments. It is not an exaggeration to say that in 1918 the Bolshevik government had not one country in the world that was friendly towards it. The reasons for this were many. Firstly, the Bolsheviks had come to power by means of violence and were preachers of world revolution—it was not considered possible to have normal diplomatic relations with such a government. Secondly, the Bolsheviks had aroused the hostility of the allies by taking Russia out of the war against Germany in a crucial year. Thirdly, the Bolsheviks did not look as if they would respect the various debts to western countries incurred by Tsarist governments. Fourthly, the methods used by the Bolsheviks in stamping out opposition horrified many people in the west. In 1918, too, there were few observers of the Russian scene who were willing to predict the life of the new régime as being more than a few months. It seemed more sensible to many governments to establish relations with the various white leaders rather than with the Bolsheviks. Even by the end of 1920 when the new régime had overcome its internal opponents the majority of countries were loth to establish diplomatic relations.

It was this feeling of isolation that drew Russia towards Germany. Germany, smarting under what it felt to be the injustices of Versailles, also saw in the Soviet a temporary ally who could help her to overcome some of the military clauses of the peace settlement. In 1922 Russia and Germany signed the Treaty of Rapallo. This Treaty provided for friendship between Russia and Germany, and for the military training by Russia of selected groups of German soldiers and airmen. This uneasy alliance of Germany and Russia continued until Hitler's rise to power.

Between 1920 and 1929 Russia slowly began to re-establish diplomatic relations with the rest of the world. There were a number of factors which helped her to achieve this. Firstly, by the mid-twenties it had become obvious that the Bolshevik government was fairly firmly planted in power, and that a refusal to recognize it in the hope that it would be supplanted by a more acceptable régime was unrealistic. Secondly, many western countries hoped by re-establishing diplomatic relations to bring about trade with the Soviet and some discussion of Tsarist debts. Thirdly, though, and perhaps the most important reason for the willingness to recognize the Soviet government was that by the end of the 'twenties Soviet 'world revolution' propaganda had subsided, and the Bolsheviks appeared to be concentrating more on achieving a planned society at home than on fomenting revolutions abroad.

By 1929 the Soviet had diplomatic relations with every major country in the world except America. In 1932 she signed non-aggression pacts with France and Italy. By 1933 with Hitler's final rise to power France had come to look upon Russia as a possible ally against Germany. During this period Japanese ambitions in the Pacific were worrying both America and Russia, and these mutual fears led to a *rapprochement*—America recognized the Soviet Union and supported Russia's entry in 1934 into the League of Nations. It was during the 'thirties, too, that left-wing sympathizers in other countries of the Soviet system carried on a ceaseless campaign to arouse public support for her.

World attention was riveted on Russia in the late nineteen-thirties because of the great purges which took place there.

Between 1934 and 1939 about 200,000 Communist Party members were expelled in Russia and thousands of others executed or imprisoned. Amongst these, for instance, were:

All the members of Lenin's first post—revolution Politbureau (the Soviet inner cabinet of 1917), with the exception of Stalin.

Three out of five Marshals of the Soviet Army, and some 30,000 Soviet officers.

Nine out of eleven cabinet ministers holding office in 1936.

Various accusations were made against the above, counter revolution and espionage for Germany being the main ones. These accusations masked the real reason for the trials—Stalin's determination to root out all opposition to his personal dictatorship.

The period 1933 to 1941 saw Russia and Germany manœuvring for what both knew would finally be a bitter struggle. Hitler described himself as the defender of Europe against Bolshevism, while the Russian Communists had analysed Fascism as being a militant form of counter revolution. In 1937 the Spanish Civil War broke out when General Franco and the Spanish army set out to overthrow the left-wing Republican government. Germany and Italy actively supported Franco, while Russia gave what assistance she could to the Republicans. Spain became a testing ground for many of the weapons that were later to be used in the Second World War.

In 1938 occurred the Munich crisis over Czechoslovakia. Hitler demanded the cession by the Czechs of the western part of their territory called the Sudetenland which was mainly populated by people of German descent. Chamberlain from Britain, Daladier from France and Mussolini from Italy met Hitler at Munich to try to resolve the problem. Russia at this time was very active in trying to organize a united front of countries against Hitler's demands, and her view that a stand should be made against Hitler over Czechoslovakia met with

Soviet Foreign Relations

a good deal of support in Britain and France. The Munich agreement, however, gave Germany the Sudetenland. Chamberlain was heavily criticized afterwards for what many considered an act of treachery against the Czechs, but he felt that Britain was in no position in 1938 to take her differences with Germany to the point of war.

The period 1938 to 1941 saw Russia trying to improve her defensive position. She absorbed the small Baltic states of Latvia, Lithuania and Estonia, and occupied the eastern areas of Poland when Hitler attacked Poland in September 1939. Russia also forced Rumania to give her Bessarabia. In 1940 she attempted, in very cold-blooded fashion, to crush the Finns, who although they resisted valiantly were forced to cede Karelia near Leningrad.

In 1939 Germany and Russia signed a non-aggression pact that astounded the world. Germany had no intention of keeping the pact and probably regarded it as a means of ensuring peace in the east while she crushed France. In 1941 Germany attacked Russia and the battle between Fascist and Communist dictatorship began.

READING LIST

The Theory and Practice of Communism, R. N. Carew Hunt (Bles).

The Soviet Union, G. Jorré (Longmans).

Soviet Trade Unions, I. Deutscher (Royal Institute of International Affairs).

The Bolshevik Revolution, 1917–1923, E. H. Carr (Macmillan).

Stalin: A Political Biography, I. Deutscher (Oxford).

The Russian Peasant and Other Studies, Sir John Maynard (Gollancz).

Lost Splendour, Prince Felix Youssoupoff (Cape).

The Invisible Writing, A. Koestler (Collins).

Chapter Three

THE UNITED STATES OF AMERICA

When the First World War broke out America wanted to stay neutral. She had never played a prominent part in international affairs and the majority of politically conscious Americans preferred to remain uninvolved in Europe's troubles as long as European powers did not interfere or question American supremacy in the western hemisphere.[1] This desire of America for neutrality was finally made impossible by German submarine policy. In 1917 the Germans determined on a policy of unrestricted submarine warfare—Britain was to be brought to her knees by sinking every ship, of whatever nationality, carrying supplies to her. These indiscriminate sinkings involved a number of American ships, and because protests to Germany did not receive any lasting satisfaction America declared war in April. This declaration of war was brought about not only by the anger aroused by the cold-blooded murder of Americans, but also by a growing sympathy for the Allied cause. An increasing number of Americans began to feel that a policy of neutrality which might sway the fortunes of the war in favour of Germany was not to America's interest. By October 1918 1,750,000 American troops were in France, and American manpower would have

[1] In 1823 President Monroe issued the famous declaration, which bears his name, warning European powers that the American continent must not be considered territory for European colonisation. The declaration was framed largely on the advice of Jefferson who had written 'Our first and fundamental maxim should be, never to entangle ourselves in the broils of Europe. Our second, never to suffer Europe to intermeddle with cis-Atlantic affairs.' This outlook on foreign affairs was still most prevalent in the United States as late as 1914.

The United States of America

been a decisive factor in the war if Germany had attempted a long resistance.

One of the leading American internationalists was the Democratic Party President, Woodrow Wilson. Wilson hoped that American entry into the war was the beginning of a new chapter in his country's history, and that she would from now on play a prominent part in world affairs as a force for peace and the defence of democratic ideals. Wilson did not share Clemenceau's bitter feelings about Germany and even as late as January 1918 still hoped for a negotiated peace with the Central Powers. Wilson attempted to be a moderating force at the Versailles discussions, and although the Treaty was far harsher than he wished, Wilson managed to prevent French occupation of the Rhineland and tried to moderate reparation demands. Before he became President of the United States in March 1913 Wilson had been a university professor of political science and believed passionately in translating the democratic and liberal ideals underlying his teaching into political practice. Wilson believed the war represented the triumph of democratic ideas over despotism and was optimistic about the future. During the closing months of the war Wilson was active in formulating the principles on which the League of Nations should be based and may be described as the League's main architect. Wilson's concept of the League was of a great body of democratic nations discussing their differences in an atmosphere of compromise and tolerance, and active and co-operative in solving the outstanding social and economic problems of the world. In this great new organization he expected America to play a prominent part. Finally, however, although he remained in office as President until 1921, Wilson failed to get America to join the League. To understand the reasons for his failure we must know something of the American system of government.

PRESIDENT AND SENATE

The American system of government is based upon the

63

The United States of America

Constitution drawn up in 1787 and the various amendments passed since this date.[1] America is a federal country, consisting now of forty-eight states, with a central government in Washington looking after national affairs and enjoying those powers not reserved for the individual states. The American central legislature is called Congress and consists of two chambers—the House of Representatives and the Senate. The House of Representatives, the lower House, is elected every two years by a system of almost complete universal suffrage (some negroes are debarred from the vote in a number of southern states on grounds of illiteracy); for this purpose the country is divided into constituencies, the more populous states such as Rhode Island having more representatives than sparsely populated states such as New Mexico. The Senate, the upper House, was designed by the founders of the United States to represent equally the interests of the various states in the central government. There are now ninety-six senators, two from each of the forty-eight states. Senators serve for a six-year term and are elected by the voters in their particular state,[2] the arrangement being that one third of the senators retire every two years. The head of the executive in America—the man who ensures that laws passed by Congress are implemented—is the President. A Supreme Court was also established to protect the Constitution and adjudicate in disputes over the meaning of its provisions.

The Supreme Court is the highest court in the nation. Its decisions are final and there is no other court to which appeal can be made from it. The Chief Justice and his eight Associate Justices who sit in the Court are appointed by the President with the approval of the Senate.

The American President has very great powers, which may be summarized as follows:

1. He makes an annual 'State of the Union' address to Con-

---

[1] Twenty-two amendments to the Constitution were passed between 1787 and 1953, of which the 21st (1933) repealed the 18th (1918 Prohibition).

[2] Before 1913 (17th amendment) they were chosen by the state legislatures.

gress and can use this speech to initiate a personal political programme and influence the type of legislation passed by Congress.

2. He will be the leader of one of the two main American parties—the Democrats or the Republicans—and will play an important part in formulating his party's policy.

3. He has a veto on legislation passed by Congress and unless legislation he has vetoed receives a two-thirds majority on returning to Congress, it is nullified.

4. He is Commander-in-Chief of the armed forces and appoints to the highest posts in the federal government.

5. He is also responsible for the conduct of foreign affairs although all treaties must be ratified by two thirds of the Senate.

A number of forces, however, work against the President's freedom to make full use of these powers granted him by the Constitution. Many Presidents, for instance, have had long battles with the Supreme Court who have interpreted many of their policies as 'unconstitutional'. The greatest check to a President's freedom of action is that his party may not enjoy a majority in Congress through the whole of his four-year term. In Britain we have what is called a Parliamentary executive. By this we mean the Prime Minister and his cabinet must have a majority behind them in the most important body of the legislature, the House of Commons. If the executive in Britain loses the support of the Commons, as Mr Chamberlain did in 1940, then it will fall from power. In America, on the other hand, we have what is called a fixed, or non-Parliamentary executive. The President is elected separately by the people and does not come into office by the victory of his party in an election. Elections for the Houses of Congress take place on different occasions from the election of a President and, because the political allegiances of the electorate can rapidly change, we often have the situation in America of a President not enjoying a majority of support throughout the two Houses of Congress. The President is elected to office for a period of four years. Half-way through his term of office elections take place for the House of Representatives and for one third of the seats in the Senate. Thus, even if the President's party had a majority throughout Congress when he was elected, he may well find that during the second half of his term he has lost the support of one, or even both, Houses of Congress.

We are now in a position to understand why Woodrow Wilson finally failed to involve America in the League. When the war ended in 1918 Wilson found that all the foreign agreements he wished to make would have to be approved by a Senate now controlled by the opposition party, the Republicans. Try as he would Wilson could not get the Senate to agree to America joining the League. Under the American Constitution all foreign treaties had to be ratified by a two-thirds majority in the Senate. The Republicans did not want America to become involved in European commitments and supported the idea of isolationism. To arouse support for his internationalism Wilson made a strenuous tour of America speaking on behalf of the League idea. If, he thought, I can get the overwhelming support of the people for American participation then the Senate will have to agree as well. In September 1919 Wilson suffered a severe stroke from which he never properly recovered—the result, we can presume, of his hectic campaigning for the League. In March 1920 the Senate finally voted for the rejection of the League Covenant. America, originally expected to be one of the leading members of the Council, was not to join the League.

American foreign policy, if such it can be called, from the failure of Wilson to the economic aid given to Britain in 1940, can be summed up by the word isolationism. During the inter-war period the Senate tended to be controlled by politicians who wanted to avoid American involvement in the problems and troubles of Europe. They believed the rest of the world should be left to 'fry in its own fat' and that America should concentrate on supremacy and development within the western Hemisphere.

WAR DEBTS CONTROVERSY

Although determined to remain politically uninvolved in the problems of Europe America could not help, because of the large sums of money she had lent her allies during the war, being interested economically in the condition of Europe. At the end of the war European private and government debts to America amounted to 12,600 million dollars. The American government pressed not only for the current interest dues on this huge sum of money but also for 'amortisation' (the repayment of the principal in regular instalments). It was also stated that America would not recognize any connection between allied debts to her and the satisfactory receipt by these countries of German reparations.

These demands created grave economic difficulties for Europe which did not even possess sufficient dollars to cover current needs from America. Britain suggested as a complete solution the cancellation of all war debts (despite the fact that Britain had lent her allies twice as much as she herself had borrowed from America). America refused to consider this radical solution but as a concession she did lower interest rates on the debts and extended the length of repayment for a number of governments.

The position at the end of 1934 was that America was still sending out formal notices to foreign debtors reminding them of the amounts due but was finding that the majority of these debtors had defaulted completely and the rest, except for Finland which paid in full, were only making token payments. In the first half of 1933, for instance, Britain received a bill for 75,950,000 dollars and paid 10,000,000 dollars; France had a bill for 40,738,567 dollars and paid nothing. By 1938 the British government was replying to debt notices with a customary declaration that it would be willing to reopen discussions, 'whenever circumstances were such as to warrant the hope that a satisfactory result might be reached.' The failure of her debtors was an important factor in America's isolationist outlook in the inter-war period.

REPUBLICAN ECONOMIC POLICY

The two main political parties in America are known as the Republicans and Democrats. The Republicans may be described as the conservatives of American political life, the Democrats the liberals. To sum up these parties in such a way can, of course, be very misleading. Some elements today, for instance, among the Democrats—the 'Dixiecrats'—are very reactionary in many matters such as negro rights. On the whole, however, we can say that the Republicans have regarded most government interference with a good deal of suspicion. Democratic administrations, on the other hand, have introduced many welfare schemes and been far less hesitant in interfering with the activities of private business, where they have considered this desirable.

In 1920 the Republican Harding was elected President.[1] In the immediate post-war period the Republicans were returned with large majorities in elections and Harding was in a powerful position to implement the party's policy. The Republicans believed that the government must not interfere with the workings of private business; it was the government's task to concentrate on giving the American economic system a fillip in the direction of expansion and high profits:

'Fostered by the general prosperity which prevailed at least in the urban areas of the country, the tone of American government policy during the twenties was eminently conservative. It was based upon the belief that if government did what it could to foster the welfare of private business, prosperity would trickle down to all ranks of the population."[2]

[1] The Presidential election of that year saw American women voting for the first time—they were given the franchise by the 19th amendment to the Constitution passed in June 1919.

[2] *An Outline of American History.* chapter VIII. 'America In The Modern World.' United States Information Service.

Republican Economic Policy

Various measures were taken by the Republicans in their policy of helping private business:

1. Tariff Acts against foreign goods were passed in 1922 and 1930. These placed very high import duties on many foreign articles that were also produced at home by American firms. High tariff barriers against foreign goods guaranteed to American manufacturers a virtual monopoly in many fields of the domestic market. This measure appeared very beneficial for a short period but resulted in the end in many foreign countries erecting similar tariff barriers against American goods. The Tariff Acts also had unpleasant repercussions on American agriculture (see below).

2. During the war years taxation on higher incomes had considerably increased. Andrew Mellon, the Secretary of the Treasury in Harding's government, believed the rich should be given more opportunity to invest in private industry and stimulate its expansion. Between 1921 and 1929, therefore, a series of laws were passed by Congress reducing income tax and excess profits tax.

3. Towards the end of the war, because of military needs, a number of enterprises had been placed under strict government control and Harding now decided to return these to full private control. In 1920, for instance, the Transportation Acts were passed which restored the railroads to private management. Between 1917 and 1920 the Merchant Marine had been owned and mainly operated by the government, and this also was sold back to private persons.

During the twenties Republican policy did appear to stimulate American industry and there was something of a boom period in company profits. As we shall see when discussing the slump, however, this period already contained the seed of impending economic disaster. Throughout the twenties in the field of agriculture Harding's tariff measures against foreign

The United States of America

goods led to bankruptcy for many farmers. Countries which previously bought foodstuffs from America relied on their exports to pay for them and when their goods could no longer enter the American market at competitive prices their purchases of American foodstuffs fell accordingly.

AMERICAN MATERIALISM

American society in the twenties was obsessed with material values. A person's standing in the eyes of his fellows depended largely upon the size of his income and possessions. Ostentation was the order of the day. Many American intellectuals reacted against these prevailing values. Writers such as H. L. Mencken and Scott Fitzgerald analysed what they considered to be this sickness of the society around them. Sinclair Lewis in his *Main Street* and *Babbitt* satirized the contemporary criteria of success. Some Americans, suffering from ennui at the brashness of their own society, preferred to live in Europe where they believed there was a greater opportunity to concentrate on intellectual pursuits. In the inter-war years a permanent colony of emigre American artists was to be found in Paris. Most of the early work of Ernest Hemingway, for instance, was produced in Europe. Somerset Maugham's character Larry in *The Razor's Edge* is an interesting portrait of a typical well-off American of the period who preferred to travel the world searching for an acceptable philosophy of life rather than enjoy the easily acquired success of inheriting and running the family business. The reaction of these intellectuals at the arid materialism of American society in the twenties did reflect the uneasiness of many Americans at the excessive emphasis on individualism and competitiveness.

American society during this period was also marked by a great amount of corruption in public life. A few cities, such as Chicago, actually fell for a time under the control of gangs of crooks who engineered city elections in favour of their own nominees. The activities of these crooks received an impetus from the Eighteenth amendment to the Constitution passed in

American Materialism

1919. This laid down that the sale or transport of alcoholic drinks in the United States was an offence. The consumption of alcoholic drinks was prohibited. American prohibition is a glaring example of how a law can only be really effective in so far as it does not conflict with the settled habits and opinions of the people it is meant to serve. It is doubtful whether the majority of Americans were ever in favour of prohibition, and crooks soon found added source of income in peddling drink and running 'speakeasies' where illicit bars functioned. Finally this law became so openly violated that in 1933 the 21st amendment to the Constitution was passed repealing prohibition.

RESTRICTION ON IMMIGRATION

In 1920 the population of America was nearly 106 million. During the preceding century nearly 30 million immigrants had entered the country from the continent of Europe alone. In 1924 the Republican administration felt that some restriction should now be placed on further immigration and in that year passed the Immigration Quota Law. This limited the annual intake to 150,000 which was to be distributed among nationalities in proportion to the number of their countrymen already in America in 1920. The period of westward expansion was over. All the territory of the Union was now opened up and there did not seem to be the need for such large numbers of immigrants as formerly. When admitting immigrants every attempt was made to ensure that America's reputation as a political asylum for the persecuted was maintained. Many refugees from Europe's fascist dictatorships, such as the philosopher Einstein and the writer Remarque, were admitted and a number of these eventually became American citizens. After 1945 America became a refuge for opponents of Communism who had escaped from their own country.

SLUMP

In 1929 the beginnings of a world slump appeared in America. A slump may be defined as a contraction of economic life and

The United States of America

during the next four years the major industrial countries of the world found increasing difficulty in selling goods both internally and externally, unemployment soared and a general panic arose about the security of investments. The slump came as a complete surprise to most Americans. In 1928 there had been a great deal of activity in the buying and selling of shares in Wall Street, the American stock market. The following year it suddenly became very difficult to sell shares, confidence in investments collapsed and people began to clamour to realize the value of their shares—the famous Wall Street crash had occurred. American industry had to sack many employees and this led to a decrease in the purchasing power of consumers which in turn led to more unemployment. By 1931 unemployment had shot to 15 million:

> 'During the 'twenties, it seemed as if prosperity would go on for-ever; even after the stock market crash in the fall of 1929, optimistic predictions continued to come from high places. But the depression deepened rapidly and steadily; the economic life of the country spiralled dizzily downward, millions of investors lost their life savings, business houses closed their doors, factories shut down, banks crashed, and millions of unemployed walked the streets bitterly in a hopeless search for work. In American national experience, there had been nothing except the long-forgotten depression of the 1870's to compare with this.'[1]

Leading economists devoted much research to analysing the reasons for slumps and produced a variety of theories most of which threw some light on the question. Lord Keynes claimed that slumps were caused by rapidly rising production without a corresponding rise in consumption—purchasers were not earning enough wages to buy all the goods being produced. High tariffs were also claimed as the evil—import duty on foreign goods led to reprisals abroad and exports fell, so that

[1] *An Outline of American History.* Chapter VIII 'America In The Modern World.' United States Information Service.

unemployment was the result. Increasing mechanization was possibly another cause of the slump in that it led to a smaller labour force being necessary in some industries and so to unemployment. The failure of the Republicans to tackle the depression energetically brought about their fall from office. A period of Democratic Party ascendancy over both the legislature and Presidency began in 1932 and lasted for twenty years.

The candidates in the Presidential election of 1932 were the Republican Herbert Hoover and the Democrat Franklin Delano Roosevelt, Governor of New York. The pivot of the election was obviously the candidate's attitudes to the slump, then at its most serious. In his speeches Hoover argued that the slump was part of a world economic cycle that would soon right itself provided governments did not interfere with the working of private business. The depression, Hoover claimed, was an unpleasant interregnum in what was to be a long period of prosperity. Roosevelt and the Democrats, on the other hand, supported a far more positive approach to the economic problems of the day. Roosevelt spoke of a 'New Deal' for all those who had suffered because of the slump. The electorate were tired of Republican inertia and Roosevelt was elected with a handsome majority—Roosevelt got 22,800,000 votes to Hoover's 15,700,000.

Franklin Delano Roosevelt (1882–1945): Franklin Delano Roosevelt was born in Duchess county, New York, the only son of James Roosevelt a business man. President Theodore Roosevelt was a distant cousin. Roosevelt graduated at Harvard in 1904 and then studied law at Columbia University. While at Columbia he married a distant cousin Eleanor Roosevelt who was later justly to achieve fame in her own right as a writer and delegate to the United Nations Assembly. In 1910 and 1912 he was elected to the Senate as a Democrat and was the unseccessful Democratic Vice-Presidential candidate in the 1920 election. In 1921 came a great crisis in his life when he was struck down by infantile paralysis; although he never

fully recovered from this, he determined that it must not interfere with his career. In 1928 he became Governor of New York
State and was re-elected in 1930. In 1932 Roosevelt was
nominated by the Democrats as their Presidential candidate
and his call for a 'New Deal' won him a comfortable victory.
This New Deal policy of Roosevelt in tackling the slump we
shall describe in detail below. In 1936 Roosevelt was re-elected
with a majority of 8,593,130 votes over the Republican
Landon. Roosevelt strived throughout the 'thirties to maintain
world peace, but realized much sooner than most Americans
the threat to democracy of the Axis powers. The Japanese
attack on Pearl Harbour in 1941 finally brought America
into the war. During the war years which followed Roosevelt
energetically organized the resources of America for final
victory. In 1940 he was re-elected for a third time and in 1944
for a fourth, a feat which no American will ever repeat.[1]
Roosevelt died suddenly only a few weeks before the end of the
war in Europe.

THE NEW DEAL

As soon as Roosevelt came to office in 1932 his administration
introduced measures to ease the worst features of the slump
and by 1935 as a result of Roosevelt's policy American prosperity was returning. The extreme laissez-faire which had
characterized the Republicans was abandoned and a determined effort was made to restore confidence throughout the
economic system:

1. A number of financial measures were first introduced.
   Sound banks were opened up again for business. Credit
   facilities on a more generous scale than previously were
   made available to industrialists and to farmers by new
   government agencies. To stop the withdrawal of savings
   bank deposits up to 5,000 dollars were insured by the
   government. Controls were also introduced regulating the

[1] An amendment has been approved limiting any American's tenure of
the Presidency to not more than two terms.

The New Deal

way securities could be sold on the stock exchange; this measure was designed to reduce the frantic selling of stock that was lowering confidence over the whole economic system.

2. Two methods were followed by the Democrats in helping depressed American agriculture. Firstly, money payments were made to farmers who would join in a long term agricultural programme sponsored by the government and plant soil-conserving crops. In 1940 nearly 6 million farmers were receiving federal subsidies. Secondly, farmers could borrow money from a new government agency called the Credit Commodity Corporation. In 1939 the income earned by farmers was more than double what it had been in 1932 and farmers were a prosperous body.

3. Cordell Hull, Roosevelt's Secretary of State, also began to break down the tariff barriers to world trade erected by the Republicans. Hull obtained reciprocity agreements from a number of foreign countries designed to admit their goods for a similar concession to American exports. Under the Trade Agreements Act of June 1934, Hull negotiated trade agreements with Canada, Cuba, France and Russia. Largely as a result of this new tariff policy there was a marked improvement by 1935 in the volume of American trade.

4. A number of schemes were introduced to help those who had suffered the worst effects of the depression. Provision was made, for instance, for some unemployment relief. In 1935 a Social Security Act was passed which assured a modest retirement pension to many kinds of workers at sixty-five. The Democrats also encouraged the growth of well-organized trade unions. In 1933 Labour was guaranteed the right of collective bargaining. The American Federation of Labour, the national organization of trade unions, was slow in organizing the unskilled

workers and the majority of its members were craft unionists. New unions, however soon appeared which organized all levels of skill and these new unions formed a national body called the Congress of Industrial Organizations. In 1929 only 4 million Americans were members of trade unions. By 1939 the figure was eleven million and in 1948 had increased to sixteen million. This growth of labour organization led to a development of collective bargaining and many improvements in wages and conditions for American workers.

5. Under Roosevelt the federal government also sponsored a number of area development schemes which did much to raise the living standards in a number of previously depressed or underdeveloped areas. The Tennessee Valley Authority's work, for instance, was a great social and economic experiment that became world famous. The Muscle Shoals project also deserves mention here—a great dam construction scheme which benefited a large area of Alabama.

Despite the social and economic improvements which accrued from the New Deal to many Americans, Roosevelt's policy seemed to some to be a dangerous increase in government interference in business and society and represented an undermining of democratic liberties. Roosevelt believed, however, in a new and more positive approach to a government's duties than these critics. In 1938 in a radio speech he said:

'Democracy has disappeared in several other great nations, not because the people of those nations disliked democracy, but because they had grown tired of unemployment and insecurity, of seeing their children hungry while they sat helpless in the face of government confusion and government weakness through lack of leadership in government. Finally, in desperation, they chose to sacrifice liberty in the hope of getting something to eat. We in America know that our democratic institutions can be preserved and made

The New Deal

to work. But in order to preserve them we need . . . to prove that the practical operation of democratic government is equal to the task of protecting the security of the people. The people of America are in agreement in defending liberties at any cost, and the first line of the defence lies in the protection of economic security.'

THE END OF ISOLATION

Probably the majority of Americans wished to remain uninvolved in the problems of Europe and Asia in the thirties. Many of them still felt that America could avoid entanglement provided she maintained a policy of strict neutrality. Between 1935 and 1937 the Neutrality Legislation passed by Congress prohibited trade or credit to any belligerent. Roosevelt and Hull did not agree with this policy. Roosevelt considered that the struggle looming between democracy and totalitarianism to be too vital for America to remain a mere interested spectator. When France fell Americans, although still opposed to actual American entry into the war, were willing to send beleagured Britain war material on a lease lend basis. On December 7th 1941 the Japanese attack on Pearl Harbour, the main American naval base in the Pacific, brought America into the struggle against the fascist powers. Once involved in the war Americans made an all out effort for victory and American manpower and military equipment were to prove one of the decisive factors in the victory against the Axis. On January 6th 1942, shortly after American entry into the war, Roosevelt called for the production during the coming year of 60,000 aircraft, 45,000 tanks, 20,000 anti-aircraft guns and eighteen million deadweight tons of merchant shipping. The treacherous Japanese attack on Pearl Harbour spelled the end of American isolationism. Roosevelt died shortly before the war ended and was succeeded by his Vice-President, Harry S. Truman. Truman represented America at the Potsdam Conference with Russia and Britain at the end of the war.

The United States of America

When the war ended America began a rapid process of demobilization and disarmament. By 1947, however, America along with the other western democracies had come to the conclusion that there was a real threat to peace from Russia. The majority of Americans realized by now that it was impossible to return to the isolationism of the 'thirties. America played a leading part in helping Europe to economic recovery, the rearmament of the democracies and the foundation in 1949 of the North Atlantic Treaty Organization.

THE AMERICAN NEGRO

The battle of ideas since the end of the war between democracy and communism has led many Americans to give their attention to the ethical weaknesses of American society today. Chief among these problems is the position of the Negro in American life. Some Americans have considered that the treatment of the Negro is the greatest weakness in their moral position when arguing with critics of democracy. Professor S. Warren in his *Ferment On The Race Question* voiced this view:

> 'In no other area is there such a contrast between the American creed, the American ideal, the American dream on the one hand, and the American reality on the other. A wide gulf separates the ideals by which American men and women live and the actual state of affairs. That, it seems to me, is the great American tragedy of the present time.'[1]

Discrimination against Negroes is completely out of keeping with the intentions of the founders of the Union[2] and yet this

[1] Professor S. Warren. *Ferment on the Race Question.* United States Information Service 1951.

[2] The Declaration of Independance of July 4th 1776 reads:
'We hold these truths to be self-evident, that all men are created equal; that they are endowed by their Creator with certain inalienable rights; that among these are life, liberty, and the pursuit of happiness. That to secure these rights, governments are instituted among men, deriving their just powers from the consent of the governed; that, whenever any form of government becomes destructive of these ends, it is the right of the people to alter or abolish it, and to institute a new government, laying its foundation on such principles, and organising its powers in such form, as to them shall seem most likely to effect their safety and happiness.'

discrimination still persists. In 1950 there were over fourteen million Negroes living in America. Two thirds of the Negro population live in the southern states and it is in these states that the grosser forms of racial discrimination exist. In some of these states Negroes must buy railway tickets at a separate ticket window from whites, buses contain Negro seat sections, bars have 'whites only' signs and the majority of universities will not register Negroes for first degrees. South Carolina as late as 1954 still had a law requiring segregation of Negroes in all factories. Despite the fact that there are many successful Negroes in America[1] the bulk of America's coloured population remains a very depressed class still suffering from much discrimination.

TECHNICAL AND ECONOMIC PROGRESS

The sections on the slump in this chapter must not be allowed to obscure the underlying cumulative achievements of technical and economic progress in America over the last half century. This development has been founded on the abundance of raw materials within her frontiers and a large and highly intelligent labour force. It has taken place, however, only because of the efficiency consciousness of management in American industry and the pioneering of a number of American industrialists. We must mention here as an outstanding example of these men the great automobile king, Henry Ford.

Henry Ford (1863–1947): Henry Ford was born near Dearborn in the State of Michigan. As a young man he experimented on his father's farm in the manufacture of a steam tractor. In 1892 he produced his first motor-car—a two cylinder 4 h.p.—and in 1899 went into the automobile business. Then he formed the Ford Motor Company which in 1909 produced the standard 'T' model which became famous throughout the world. By 1930 Ford had put over 20,000,000

---

[1] We can mention the following: Ralph Bunche statesman, Dr Alain Locke philosopher, Ralph Ellison novelist, Marion Anderson contralto, Edith Sampson diplomat, Charles Drew surgeon, and Louis Armstrong jazz.

cars on the road and was employing a quarter of a million persons. In 1924 he founded his largest factory abroad at Dagenham where between 1931 and 1946 over 1,000,000 vehicles were manufactured. Ford's industrial empire yielded him an immense fortune, but money was never his main spur.

AMERICA'S ECONOMIC STRENGTH

One of the biggest factors in the world struggle between democracy and communism is the economic strength of America:

1. America is rich in natural resources. There is hardly a raw material which is not found within her borders and those she lacks could, in an emergency, be totally replaced by substitutes.

2. America in 1953 had a population of over 150 million people giving her a huge labour force. This labour force is well educated and contains a high proportion of well-trained technicians.

3. America's industrial production in 1950 was 94 per cent greater than in 1939 and her industrial plant is being increased daily. To produce her industrial products America mined in 1950 ninety million tons of iron ore, 800,000 tons of copper, 400,000 tons of lead, 600,000 tons of zinc and 500 million tons of coal.

4. No less than 60 per cent of America's land was being farmed in 1950—403 million acres. Thirty-five per cent of this farmland grew crops in 1950 equal to the combined crop production of France, Germany, Italy, the Netherlands and Belguim. In 1948 nearly twenty-two million tons of foodstuffs were exported—a record. Along with this increase in her food exports Americans themselves are eating better than ever before—domestic food consumption in 1950 was 10 per cent above the 1939 rate.

5. America's merchant fleet has also increased rapidly. In 1939 her merchant fleet consisted of 1,091 ships totalling

9,300,000 tons. In 1950 the fleet had increased to 1,212 ships totalling 14,550,000 tons.

Without the economic power of America the west would have been in a hopeless position in 1947 when it set out to achieve military security.

READING LIST

The Epic of America, J. T. Adams (Routledge).

The U.S.A.: An Outline of the Country, Its People and Institutions, D. W. Brogan (Oxford).

America's Economic Strength, C. J. Hitch (Oxford).

T.V.A., D. E. Lilienthal (Penguin Books).

The American Political System, D. W. Brogan (Hamilton).

The Story of the American People, C. F. Strong (Hodder and Stoughton).

Chapter Four

THE FASCIST POWERS

The Peace Settlement reached in the various treaties signed between 1919 and 1923 was only to last twenty years and this short period was to be, as Professor Carr has described it, a twenty-year crisis. The end of the 1914–1918 'war to end wars', far from bringing an era of peace and international friendship as had been hoped, proved merely to be the beginning of recurring international crises which finally precipitated the 1939–1945 war. The purpose of this chapter is to describe these crises and to analyse the three countries—Germany, Italy and Japan—whose aggressions eventually led to the second world war. During the war these countries were collectively described as the fascist powers and it was presumed that their régimes had some common factors. At the end of the chapter we shall try to outline these common factors.

GERMANY

GERMANY IN 1919

In November 1918 the Kaiser, realizing the war was lost and frightened by allied talk of hanging 'war criminals', abdicated and fled to Holland. A moderate socialist government was formed in Berlin and an ex-saddler named Ebert became the first President of the new German Republic. In the months immediately following the end of the war Germany was in a turmoil. The Allied blockade had brought the population to near starvation, the new government had not consolidated its administration, it seemed likely that the Allies would march into Germany at any minute, and, along with these troubles, revolutionaries released from imprisonment were conspiring to establish a communist dictatorship.

In January 1919 these German communists led by Karl Liebknecht and Rosa Luxembourg seized Berlin. Events in Germany at this period are reminiscent of Russia during 1917. When Kerensky's liberal government had come into power in the first Russian Revolution, opponents of Tsarism had been released from jail. These revolutionaries shortly afterwards overthrew Kerensky and established a Bolshevik government. In Germany these opponents of the Kaiser's government also immediately set about conspiring to overthrow the socialist government that had released them. In Germany, however, unlike Russia, they were not able to retain power and after a few days Ebert's government was once more in control in Berlin.

In February 1919 elections were held in Germany to elect 400 members for a constituent assembly to meet at Weimar. This Weimar Assembly had two main tasks—firstly, to provide the new republic with a constitution and, secondly, to sign a peace treaty with the Allies. The election returned an overwhelming majority of monarchists who had supported the war. Realizing that it would only incur Allied displeasure to restore the monarchy these conservatives drew up a new republican constitution laying down that in future Germany would be governed by democratic principles. Although most of the Assembly were also nationalists they realized that Germany was in no position at this point to resist the Versailles Treaty, and so the heavy territorial losses were complied with.

DIFFICULTIES OF THE WEIMAR REPUBLIC

We have already described how the new republican régime in January 1919 had survived an assault from the extreme left. In 1920 she faced a threat from the extreme right. Many monarchists could not reconcile themselves to the idea of a republic even if only as a temporary measure. Incensed also by the Versailles Treaty they determined to seize power, restore the monarchy, and energetically pursue a policy of resisting the Versailles Treaty. The leader of this attempted *coup d'etat* was a monarchist called Kapp, and his seizure of Berlin in 1920 has gone down to history as the Kapp Putsch, a German word meaning a quick forceful seizure of political power. Although they had lost their capital the legitimate government, however, had not despaired of routing Kapp and his associates. They called a general strike of German workers and the success of this forced Kapp to retire from Berlin to Stuttgart where his movement quickly fizzled out. The Weimar Republic had, therefore, survived attacks from both German political extremes, but difficulties with the Allies were now to face it.

The Versailles Treaty laid down that Germany should make reparations payments to the Allies. Although the reparations clauses in the Treaty were not very specific regarding the amount due from Germany the sum of £8,000,000,000 was mentioned in the Versailles meetings. In 1921 this sum was increased to the fantastic figure of £11,000,000,000 and Germany began to make monthly payments to the Allies. In 1922 Germany defaulted in her payments. The reparations clauses of the Versailles Treaty have been heavily criticized—the sum demanded was absurdly large and could only lead to the ruination of Germany, one of Europe's most important economic units. When Germany defaulted, France however, insisted that the payments must be made good and sent her troops in to occupy the Ruhr valley. The German government immediately organized a general strike in the Ruhr aimed at ensuring that France would not benefit from her occupation of Germany's main industrial centre. Although the strike to a certain extent did have this effect it was to prove the ruin of Germany.

Germany had suffered from inflation ever since the end of the war and the position became rapidly aggravated by the loss of production from the Ruhr. By inflation we mean a condition where the value of a country's currency falls rapidly because few goods and services can be bought with it. This German inflation of 1922 ruined hundreds of thousands of Germans living on fixed incomes and made the savings accounts of many virtually worthless. Faith in the mark disappeared.

It was during the unrest caused by this inflation that Germany first heard of Adolf Hitler, who made his first appearance as a political figure in 1923. Hitler, an Austrian by birth and an ex-corporal of the German army, detested the democratic Weimar régime. Impressed by Mussolini's seizure of Rome in 1922 he became a leading figure in the National Socialist Party (Nazi Party). With his supporters, including Ludendorff, the German supreme commander of the First World War, Hitler planned to seize Munich the capital of Bavaria and later to march on Berlin. The German Republic was to be destroyed and replaced not by a restored monarchy but by a dictatorship of Hitler's own party. The putsch proved a fiasco. Hitler was arrested by the Bavarian authorities and sentenced to five years imprisonment. After only serving a few months of this sentence he was released and spent this short period in beginning his book, the bible of Nazism, *Mein Kampf* (My Struggle). For a number of years yet the world was merely to laugh at the antics of the little man with the Chaplin moustache and peculiar salute.

STRESEMANN

After the French occupation of the Ruhr Germany realized that she would have to follow a careful policy towards the Allies if she was to avoid fresh humiliations. In 1923 Stresemann, leader of the nationalists, became German Chancellor (the equivalent of our Prime Minister). Stresemann set himself three aims. Firstly, he wished to effect some rapprochment with France that would lead to the evacuation of the Ruhr. Secondly, he decided to try and obtain German admission to the Council of the League which would add to Germany's prestige and allow her to claim treatment as a first-rate power. Thirdly, Stresemann hoped to amend the reparations clause of the Versailles Treaty and drastically reduce the amounts of money demanded by the allies. As soon as he took office Stresemann began to apply himself energetically to the realization of these three aims—the Ruhr strike was called off, Germany took the initiative in suggesting a meeting with her creditors to discuss the subjects of reparations, and a beginning was made in stabilizing the value of the mark and regaining people's confidence in the German currency.

Stresemann's actions created a certain degree of good feeling towards Germany among the allies. Those who had claimed that Germany had no intention of meeting her debts seemed to be proved wrong. Stresemann came to be accepted as a sincere German statesman who wished to found good relations between his country and her former enemies. Records of some of Stresemann's personal opinions at this time seem to suggest today that he was not as sincere as the optimists hoped and, in fact, that he was merely playing for time while Germany recovered from the war and prepared for the next campaign. However, at the time the Allies treated Stresemann's approaches at their face value. French troops evacuated the Ruhr and in 1925 a beginning was made in the evacuation of the Rhineland. After the Treaty of Versailles was signed all Germany west of the Rhine and a strip of territory thirty miles to the east was occupied by allied troops as security for France. It was decided that one third of this area was to be evacuated in 1925, one third in 1930 and the remainder in 1935. In 1923 France had little intention of agreeing to any evacuation, but Stresemann's protestations of friendship led her to stand by her earlier decision. Under American initiative the Allies set up the Dawes Committee (named after its American chairman General Dawes) to fix how much reparations Germany should pay each year and the convertible value of German currency in terms of the currencies of the creditor governments. America also agreed to lend Germany £40,000,000 to get this new scheme started. Meanwhile Germany's friendly overtures to neighbouring countries were bearing fruit. In 1925 the two Locarno treaties were signed by Germany. The first treaty was signed with France and

Belgium and guaranteed the 1925 frontiers of these countries, with Britain and Italy as witnesses to the agreement. The second Locarno treaty was signed with Poland and Czechoslovakia and also guaranteed their existing frontiers which were not to be altered except by general agreement—France was a witnessing signatory to this treaty. In 1926 Germany was also brought into the League of Nations, though not, as Stresemann originally hoped, as a full member of the Council; however it was still a great diplomatic victory for her. The three years from 1923 to 1926 under Stresemann's leadership had brought about a great improvement in Germany's position.

HITLER'S RISE TO POWER

The chancellorship of Stresemann appeared by 1928 to have given the Weimar Republic a certain stability. We have described above the serious inflation which Germany suffered shortly after the war. Stresemann had great difficulty in curbing this inflation, but by 1928 confidence in the mark had been restored. Behind this façade of stability, however, still existed the deep-seated hostility of a large group of Germans to the Republic. In 1929 occurred a world economic crisis whose immediate result in Germany was to swell the ranks of the opponents of German democracy and prove the death blow of the Weimar Republic. In the chapter on America will be found an analysis of the causes of the slump, and this need not detain us again. The volume of world trade in the period 1929 to 1933 sank rapidly, purchasing power fell and unemployment spiralled. After first appearing in America the slump spread rapidly to the other major industrial countries of the world until Germany too became affected. By 1930 German unemployment had risen to over six million.

It is from this point that we can trace the phenomenal rise to power of Hitler and the Nazi Party. In spite of the economic reforms and diplomatic successes of the German government in the 'twenties the idea of a democratic republic was still foreign to many Germans. The new democracy was associated in many minds with the humiliation of Versailles and democratic roots had not struck very deep. Out of the Versailles Treaty had been bred a desire for vengeance, and Weimar foreign relations had not been aggressive enough for the nationalists. The strength of German communism also perturbed the middle class who considered a strong right-wing dictatorship as the only means of avoiding eventual communist control of Germany. The Nazis had always exploited these grievances and fears and, when the slump broke out in 1929 with its unemployment and misery, they were quick to realize the new conditions would be to their political advantage. With the slump their fortunes improved rapidly.

The number of seats in the Reichstag, the German Parliament, was 646 and the following table shows the Nazi rise to power from the election of 1924 until 1933 when, with the co-operation of their allies in the nationalist parties, they enjoyed control of the Reichstag. It will be noticed that the two worst years for the Nazi vote were 1924 and 1928, the first the year of the Dawes Plan and the second a fairly prosperous year just before the slump. In 1930 when the slump was deepening their votes increased eight times on the figure for the previous election. Economic disaster was the factor which finally destroyed the Weimar Republic.

NAZI VOTES IN REICHSTAG ELECTIONS 1924–1933

Date	Votes	Seats Obtained
May 1924	2,000,000	32
December 1924	900,000	14
1928	800,000	12
1930	6,400,000	107
July 1932	13,700,000	230
November 1932	11,700,000	196
1933	17,300,000	288

Hitler's Rise to Power

In 1932 the Republic under Chancellor Brüning was desperately trying to grapple with the economic problems of the slump by a series of economy measures which proved extremely unpopular. The aged General Hindenburg, who had become President on the death of Ebert in 1925, dismissed Brüning and appointed a nationalist Fritz von Papen as Chancellor. All Germany seemed to be clamouring for a strong figure who would energetically tackle the slump and pursue a nationalistic policy, and Hindenburg offered the chancellorship to Hitler. Hitler demanded absolute powers with this office and Hindenburg at first refused. In January 1933, however, Hitler was appointed Chancellor on his earlier conditions. The Nazis still wished to maintain a pretence of democratic practice and Hitler's associate Goering, now President of the Reichstag, dissolved Parliament and fixed a general election for the 5th March 1933. The Nazis had no intention of following democratic conventions indefinitely but they wished to give the appearance of having come to power by popular acclaim. A week before the election was due to take place, therefore, they arranged for the Reichstag buildings to be burnt down in circumstances which pointed to a communist plot. In the communist scare which followed this incident the Nazis and their nationalist allies gained a clear majority in the elections. In 1934 Hindenburg died and Hitler acquired the post of President. Before the year was out he had adopted the new title of the Führer, or supreme leader, and all democratic pretence was abandoned. The Weimar Republic was dead and Nazi dictatorship had begun.

THE NAZI LEADERS

Before going on to discuss the measures introduced by the Nazis now that they had supreme power it will be interesting to sketch briefly the background and history of some of the main Nazi leaders.

Hitler (1889–1945): It is interesting to note that when Hitler became dictator of Germany in 1933 he was still comparatively unknown outside Germany. Cartoonists had tended to treat him as an object of humour rather than as a serious danger. As late as 1929 the fourteenth edition of the *Encyclopaedia Britannica* dismissed him in only fifteen lines. Hitler was born in Austria in 1889 the illegitimate son of an elderly civil servant of the Habsburg Empire. His story before the First World War is undistinguished, although of immense psychological interest. During the war he joined the German army and was promoted to corporal winning the Iron Cross (a dubious honour as at the time the German High Command were issuing many of these decorations as a boost to morale). The end of the war left him with the conviction that the German army had been stabbed in the back by the civilian population and that it had suffered no real defeat in the field. In 1919 he joined in Bavaria a semi-military organization that was later to become the National Socialist Party. This organization was soon involved in numerous brawls with communists and liberals. In November 1923 along with General Ludendorff he attempted to seize power in Munich but the putsch was abortive and he spent a number of months in prison where a beginning was made with the bible of Nazism, *Mein Kampf*. This book was to prove a peculiar mixture of autobiography, political ideas and military tactics for the forthcoming war for German supremacy. Hitler's political philosophy, if such it can be called, is largely a rationalization of a love of power for its own sake and a desire for self-glorification. Germany, Hitler considered, had been unjustly treated at Versailles. The Germans were the core of the Nordic race which was superior to all other races. Jews, Slavs, Latins, Negroes and coloured people generally, were all of a low order and fit only for subservience. Germany must make herself the master of Europe and to achieve this she must annihilate all pernicious internal elements, particularly the Jews, and build up her military strength. The apologia for German expansion was, then, to be based on a racial theory of innate German superiority. Hitler's theories were unsound

The Nazi Leaders

and pernicious, but they quickly attracted support from a number of different quarters, often from people who thought they would quickly be able to jettison Hitler when his usefulness was over. For a start, a number of disgruntled ex-soldiers and adventurers, who felt the Weimar Republic offered them no opportunity for power, gathered round him. Then, again, a good deal of Hitler's support came from those nationalist extremists who dreamed of avenging Versailles. Many German industrialists and members of the middle class, haunted by the growth of communism, also began to look to him. In 1933 Hitler at last became dictator. By 1939 Germany had all the aspects and techniques of oppression that typify the totalitarian state. The régime hardly attempted to mask the brutality directed against opponents. A stifling censorship eradicated criticism, and propaganda and mass rallies conditioned the German mind into accepting Nazi ideas. Hitler was unable to remain satisfied by his acquisition of Austria and Czechoslovakia and his attack on Poland in September 1939 precipitated war with Britain and France. After great victories between 1939 and 1942 the war began to deteriorate for Germany. Partly aided by the propaganda value of the allied demand for unconditional surrender Hitler determined to fight to the end even if this meant the complete ruin of Germany. Towards the end of the war it became increasingly obvious that Hitler's mind was deranged. In July 1944 a number of opponents who wished to end the war attempted to assassinate him in the famous Hitler bomb plot. Hitler survived, however, and Germany suffered another year of total war before he committed suicide in the siege of Berlin in 1945.

Goering (1893–1946): Hermann Wilhelm Goering was born at Rosenheim, Bavaria in 1893. During the First World War he became a pilot and after Richtofen's death commander of that ace's famous squadron. After the war Goering was a member of the disgruntled ex-officer class violently opposed to the new democratic Germany. In 1922 he joined the Nazi movement and after the failure of the 1923 putsch fled abroad.

While living in Sweden he became a morphine addict and spent some time in a mental hospital. In 1926 he returned to Germany where Hitler's fortunes were improving. Goering was made Nazi President of the Reichstag and, it is believed, was largely responsible for the Reichstag fire outrage before the elections of March 1933. In 1934 after the foundation of the Nazi dictatorship he was appointed Prime Minister of the Reich and Minister of Aviation, being promoted to General. Goering was responsible for secretly laying the foundations of German airpower despite Versailles regulations. As Reich Minister for Foreign Affairs, to which he was appointed in 1937, Goering was active in German diplomatic manoeuvres which preceded the seizure of Austria and Czechoslovakia. During the war he was responsible for the blitz bombing of Warsaw, Rotterdam and Coventry and must also have been conscious of the deplorable state of concentration camp prisoners. Goering was an extrovert flamboyant individual and after promoting himself to Field Marshal in 1938 one of his hobbies appears to have been the design of exotic uniforms for himself. At the height of German power in Europe in 1941 Goering built up a large collection of artistic loot from the occupied territories. This loot was secreted away in his Berchtesgaden home and at the end of the war was found to be worth over £20,000,000. During the war Goering became recognized as the potential successor to Hitler, but in April 1945, when Goering had fled to Bavaria, Hitler disowned him. In 1945 Goering was placed on trail at Nuremburg by the Allies and found guilty of various crimes against humanity. Sentenced to be hanged, Goering managed to poison himself before this sentence could be carried out.

Goebbels (1897–1945): Paul Joseph Goebbels was born at Rheydt in the Rhineland in 1897. His family were of poor peasant stock but, through scholarships and very hard work, Goebbels managed eventually to study at Heidelberg University where he graduated with a Ph.D. in 1920. For a short period after this he tried to make a living as a dramatist but was quite unsuccessful. In 1922 he turned his attention to politics and became one of the chief propagandists of the National Socialist Party. In 1926 he was made Nazi leader, or Gauleiter for Berlin. A year later he founded the paper *Der Angriff* which in a short time became known as the most scurrilous German daily. In 1928 he was elected to the Reichstag and in 1933 made Minister of Propaganda in Hitler's government. In this post Goebbels used every method of lie and distortion to suit Hitler's purpose and explain German aggression. Goebbels committed suicide with Hitler in the siege of Berlin.

NAZI POWER IN GERMANY

Once Hitler assumed the title of Führer in 1933 there was little further attempt at democratic pretence by the Nazis. The chief aims of the Nazis might be summarized as follows:

1. To strengthen their position by outlawing all other political parties and eradicting their most implacable opponents, particularly communists.
2. To bring all other associations in the state, for instance the churches and trade unions, under the ultimate control of the Nazi party.
3. To implement their racial theories, particularly against the Jews.
4. To build up German military strength rapidly so as to repudiate all vestiges of the Versailles Treaty, regain the lost territories, and conquer the other great powers of Europe.

A number of decrees passed in 1933 outlawed all other political parties. Some opponents of Hitler managed to flee abroad (including the future leaders of the East German communist state set up by the Russians after the war). Most of the leaders of the German parties, however, were either executed, placed in concentration camps (Schumacher, the socialist leader, languished in a concentration camp for twelve years), or went into an uneasy retirement. Hitler did not even spare his right-wing allies, the nationalists. Hitler also decided to purge his own party of its more independent members. The cold-blooded murder of a number of leading Nazis was carried out by the S.S., the Nazi political police, and in this 'blood bath' perished the young Roehme whose wedding Hitler had attended only a short time before his murder. Hitler had received a good deal of support from German industrialists, and he had no intention of nationalizing their concerns. He made it clear, however, to both them and the German trade unions, that their interests were subordinate to Nazi policy and that the German economy was to be geared to its military needs. Hitler received a good deal of opposition from the German churches and he imprisoned many well-known clergymen, including the courageous anti-Nazi Pastor Niemöller (released by the allies from a concentration camp along with Schumacher in 1945). Nazi persecution of the Jews was to prove particularly odious to the rest of the world. The Nazi policy of murder, imprisonment and intimidation of Jews on the ground of their racial inferiority was largely actuated by a desire to confiscate Jewish property.

Hitler's policy of rapid rearmament was aided by the fact that almost from the armistice, in spite of military restrictions imposed by the the Allies, the German High Command had managed to pursue the rehabilitation of German military power. The High Command did its utmost to spread the legend that German forces had never been defeated in the field, but stabbed in the back by the cowardice of the civilian population. In 1918 as much military equipment as possible was hidden from Allied disarmament investigators. Strategy for the next war was being discussed by Von Seekt, the head of the German army, before the Versailles Treaty had been signed. In 1933 Hitler withdrew the German delegates from a disarmament conference taking place at Lausanne and in the same year brought Germany out of the League of Nations. A plebiscite (carefully arranged as all of Hitler's plebiscites to achieve a desired result) showed forty million Germans in favour of rearming as against only two million opposed. From this point German rearmament was pursued fairly openly, including the building of a large German air force. In 1935 Germany signed a naval agreement with Britain by which she was to restrict her navy to thirty-five per cent of the strength of the British navy. Hitler had no intention of keeping this agreement, however, and announced a system of national conscription the same year, although this was forbidden by the Versailles Treaty.

PROPAGANDA

One of the most important aspects of modern totalitarian régimes is their use of propaganda. By propaganda we mean the artful use, ignoring truth and falsehood, of mass communication to condition people's minds in certain intended ways. The Nazis placed great faith in propaganda and their propaganda chief Goebbels occupied an important place in the party. During the war years when things began to go badly for Germany the Nazis used every technique of propaganda they could devise to delude the German people that they would enjoy ultimate victory.

NAZI EXPANSION

Hitler's foreign policy in the thirties was directed to achieving the maximum territorial gains for Germany before actually precipitating war. Hitler repeatedly announced to the world that some new territorial gain was his 'last demand', only to press immediately afterwards for the handing over of some other territory. Under the Versailles Treaty the Rhineland was to be occupied by allied troops until 1935. The last of these troops, however, were withdrawn in 1930. At Locarno Germany had agreed to keep the area demilitarized but in 1936 in spite of this agreement Hitler ordered his troops in. In 1935 the Saar coalfields voted for their return to Germany. It was hoped in Britain and France that the reacquisition of the Rhineland and the Saar would satisfy Germany for a time, but Hitler had now cast covetous eyes on Austria.

In 1934 occurred the first attempt of Germany to occupy Austria. In that year the Austrian Chancellor Dollfuss was murdered by Austrian Nazis and the German army massed on the Austrian border. Hitler was very tempted to walk in but decided to wait because of Italian objections. Four years later in 1938, when the Axis pact had made Mussolini an ally, Germany occupied Austria and Hitler celebrated the Anschluss with an emotional speech rejoicing in the return of his homeland to the Reich. The Axis pact, which led Italy to allow Austrian incorporation in Germany, was signed in 1936 by the three fascist powers Germany, Italy and Japan. The pact was announced as providing for common action in defence of the interests of the three countries. The details of the pact were not disclosed to the world but included the strategy necessary for eventual Axis world domination.

The first opportunity for joint action in furtherance of fascist interests under the Axis pact came with the Spanish Civil War (1936–1939). In 1924 the Spanish monarch Alfonso XIII consented to the establishment of a dictatorship under a Spanish soldier Primo de Rivera. This dictatorship proved extremely unpopular and was overthrown in 1930, a more liberal régime coming into being. In 1931, largely because of Alfonso's association with Rivera, the monarchy was also overthrown and the Spanish Republic proclaimed. This Republic, which began to be increasingly controlled by communists, aroused much opposition from former supporters of the dictatorship and Spanish monarchists. In 1936 General Franco, the Spanish commander in North Africa, landed in Spain with an army largely composed of Moorish troops and began his revolt against the government which developed into a civil war. The sympathies of many people in Britain and France lay with the Republicans but the British and French governments decided on a policy of non-intervention. Germany and Italy, however, gave active support to Franco in the form of munitions and military forces. Russia did her best to aid the Republicans but distance did not allow her to send many supplies. In 1939, largely because of the Axis help given to Franco, Republican resistance suddenly collapsed. Hitler particularly welcomed Franco's victory because he hoped that in the coming struggle with Britain Franco would seize Gibraltar and close Britain's sea passage into the Mediterranean.

Although Hitler had described Austria as his last territorial demand he began to press in the summer of 1938 for the return to Germany of the Sudetenland, the western provinces of Czechoslovakia. The Czechs had built strong fortifications in this area and refused to cede the territory. The situation became tense and on September 15th 1938, Chamberlain, the British Prime Minister, flew to see Hitler at Berchtesgaden. A week later at Godesburg the two discussed the Sudetenland again. Chamberlain expected Hitler to agree to a plebiscite in the disputed area but Hitler refused saying the Sudetenland was obviously Germany territory. Without either accepting or rejecting the German demand for immediate occupation Chamberlain returned to England. War between Britain and Germany seemed imminent. Many people in Britain and France believed that this was the moment to combine with the Czechs (and possibly also, some considered, with Russia) and remain implacable in the face of German threats. Even if this meant war, it was argued, the Czechs were in a position to put up a good fight. In Munich on September 29th 1938 Chamberlain, Daladier (the French Premier), Hitler and Mussolini met to discuss the crisis. Chamberlain and Daladier did not consider their countries in a military position to risk war by refusing Hitler's demands, and also allowed themselves to believe Hitler was sincere in saying that this was his 'last territorial demand'. They agreed to German occupation of the Sudetenland and the Czechs, abandoned by their Allies, had no alternative but to surrender the territory.

The Fascist Powers

In March 1939 Hitler occupied the remainder of the country.

When Germany swallowed up the remainder of Czecho-slovakia Britain and France both hoped Hitler would now be satisfied with the rapid expansion of German territory since 1934. The occupation of the remainder of Czechoslovakia was soon followed, however, by German demands on Poland. In the Versailles Treaty the new state of Poland had been given a narrow access to the Baltic Sea which became known as the Polish Corridor. This strip of territory separated East Prussia and the free city of Danzig from the rest of Germany. Hitler now began to demand the return of the Corridor and also those western areas of Poland which contained Germans. The Poles said they would do their utmost, short of actually ceding territory, to improve relations with Germany. This was not sufficient for Hitler who was determined to destroy Poland and reunite East Prussia with the rest of Germany. In August 1939 Germany and Russia amazed the world by signing the Russo-German pact. This agreement laid down that neither country would attack the other and also contained clauses for the development of trade. At the meeting in Moscow between Stalin, Molotov and Ribbentrop, the Nazi foreign minister, discussion also took place on a possible partition of Poland. On September 1st 1939 Poland was invaded by Germany. Britain and France had both given guarantees to Poland pro-viding for assistance if she was attacked, and both countries had realized that there had to be some limit to the policy of appeasing Germany. They therefore demanded an immediate evacuation of Polish territory by German troops. Germany ignored this ultimatum and continued her offensive. On September 3rd Britain and France had no alternative but to declare war. Poland did her best to resist the Germans but a Russian invasion of her eastern areas spelled the end. By the end of the month Polish resistance had collapsed. Although Russia occupied eastern Poland largely for security reasons, this fresh invasion of Poland placed Britain and France in a delicate position. Should they now be obliged to declare war on Russia too for violating Polish territory? Fortunately, Britain and France did not take this step.

ITALY

ITALY AND THE PEACE TREATIES

In the spring of 1915 Italy entered the war on the side of the Allies. Italy declared war on the central powers not for idealistic reasons but because after secret consultations with both sides she decided more territory could be gained by selling her services to the Allies. Her motives for entering the war were, then, unblushingly for gain. At the end of the war Italy was regarded as one of the Big Five—Britain, France, America, Italy and Japan—who had mainly contributed to Allied victory and Orlando, the Italian foreign minister, went to Versailles expecting to be treated as an equal by Lloyd George, Clemenceau and Wilson. This was not to be the case. Although Italy had pinned down important Austrian armies she had inflicted no great defeats on the enemy until the closing months of the war, and Orlando found that Italian views were not receiving the attention that he originally expected. Italy hoped she would emerge from the war the dominant Adriatic and Mediterranean power. Her territorial demands at Versailles and Trianon consisted of the South Tyrol, a long strip of the Adriatic coastline as far as Zara, and an Italian protectorate over Albania. Finally, however, she was merely to receive a small area of the Tyrol, the Trieste territory and the port of Zara. On the other side of the Adriatic Serbia had also been enlarged into Yugoslavia and this new state seemed likely to contest Italy's claim to Adriatic supremacy.

Having failed to achieve her ambitions at the peace treaties, Italy began to consider herself a victim of them rather than a beneficiary. Although Italy considered herself unjustly treated by the Allies her original territorial demands were quite exorbitant. She refused to recognize this, however, and left the treaty talks feeling robbed of her rights by Britain and France.

ITALIAN DEMOCRACY

Disappointment at Italy's war gains increased the hostility of many Italians to their existing system of democracy. Democracy had never struck deep roots into Italian political life and before the First World War the Italian Premier Giolitti cynically managed elections and the Italian legislature. A united democratic Italy was only fifty years old when the 1914 war broke out and the major Italian parties, while paying lip service to democratic forms of behaviour, preferred to think of government as really being the province of the 'strong man'.

At the end of the war increasing lawlessness broke out in Italy. Strikes, political demonstrations and brawls between the militant supporters of the various parties became common. In 1919 the socialist opposition party walked out of the Italian parliament and began to talk of 'direct action', that is, attempting to acquire political power by force. In September 1920 the Milan factories were seized by the workers and this abortive communist revolt was only suppressed with great difficulty. The conservative government in office during this immediate post-war period never took strong measures to curb this violence and never energetically set about tackling the various social injustices suffered by Italian workers and peasants that were leading to much unrest. This, coupled with the general debility of Italian democracy, and the unpopularity of the régime because of its association with the 'iniquitous' peace treaties, provided the totalitarian group known as the Fascists with their opportunity to seize power.

FASCIST SEIZURE OF POWER

The blackshirt, or fascist movement, had been formed in 1919 by a former socialist called Mussolini. The original name given to the movement was Fasci di Combattimento, Fascist

Fascist Seizure of Power

Fighting Groups, and these thugs were used to intimidate socialists in the 1919 general election with the connivance of the conservative régime. The movement was largely composed of dissatisfied ex-soldiers and nationalists and enjoyed a good deal of support from wealthy industrialists and landowners who feared communism. In October 1922 Mussolini felt his party strong enough to attempt to seize power, and fascist detachments converged on Rome from various parts of the country. A number of advisers surrounding the Italian monarch, King Victor Emmanuel, advised him to declare martial law and use the army to suppress the fascists. The king, however, felt the Fascists to be too strong and made Mussolini Premier—the Fascists had come to power by a bloodless revolution.

Mussolini did not immediately destroy the outward forms of Italian democracy, and until 1925 let it appear as if he was governing constitutionally and without a desire to establish a permanent dictatorship. In 1925, however, all vestiges of democracy were swept away, opposition parties dissolved, and Mussolini assumed the title of Il Duce or dictator. By retaining the monarchy, and signing an agreement in 1929 with the Pope concerning the status of the Vatican City, Mussolini managed to gain the support of many conservatives, but to the democrats and socialists in Italy his rule meant only persecution and imprisonment.

Mussolini (1883–1945): Benito Amilcare Andrea Mussolini was born in 1883 at Varano di Costa in the province of Forli. His father was a blacksmith and the family extremely poor. Mussolini senior was an atheist and socialist and named his son after Benito Juarez, the Mexican revolutionary. Mussolini received some elementary schooling and, after working for his father for a time, entered a training college for teachers and worked for a year as a teacher. In 1902 he went to Switzerland to avoid compulsory military training. During the next twelve years he became well-known in Switzerland and Italy as an extreme socialist agitator. On the outbreak of the First

The Fascist Powers

World War Mussolini was opposed to Italian intervention, but in November 1914 he suddenly became converted to Italian entry alongside the Allies and was expelled from the Italian Socialist Party. In the same month he founded a new paper *Il Popolo d'Italia* largely financed by French socialists hoping for Italian participation in the war. When Italy entered the war in May 1915 Mussolini served for five weeks in the trenches as a Bersaglieri corporal, being injured when his mortar misfired. In these few weeks he attempted to build himself up in public eyes as a hero and his paper printed many photographs of 'Mussolini in the front line'. When the war ended Mussolini became a supporter of an authoritarian Italian state pursuing a nationalist policy, and jettisoned most of his old socialist beliefs. In 1919 he founded the fascist movement and in 1922 a successful *coup d'état* was accomplished. Support for Mussolini came from a number of different groups—political adventurers and nationalists, wealthy industrialists and landowners frightened of communism, and monarchists. On assuming power Mussolini proceeded steadily to undermine Italian democracy and the brutal murder of the socialist Matteotti ushered in a period of intimidation and imprisonment for his opponents. In 1926 Mussolini attempted to secure Catholic support for his régime by signing the Lateran Treaty with the Pope giving sovereignty to the Vatican City in Rome. Italian fascism was fundamentally similar to Nazism in its emphasis on authority and nationalism. In 1936 Mussolini signed the Axis agreement with Germany and in 1940, when he considered German victory certain, Italy entered the war as Hitler's ally. In July 1943, however, Allied troops had landed on the Italian mainland from Sicily and Mussolini was overthrown and arrested by the king and a group of disgruntled Fascists. Imprisoned in the Abruzzi Mountains he was rescued by the Germans and spent the rest of the war as puppet dictator of North Italy. In April 1945 he was captured by Italian partisans and executed. For the last three years of his life Mussolini was a sick man and after his overthrow he appeared to become almost indifferent to his fate.

MUSSOLINI'S AGGRESSIONS

Mussolini's intention was, as he expressed it himself, to make the Mediterranean 'an Italian lake'. He dreamt of Italy becoming the dominant power in the Mediterranean area and saw Britain and France as his main opponents in this policy of expansion. Italy, Mussolini considered, had been harshly treated at the peace settlement and needed more territory for her expanding population. The Italian colonies in Africa—Libya, Somaliland and Eritrea—were poor in resources and Mussolini soon cast envious eyes on the French colony of Tunisia and British-controlled Egypt. When Hitler first came to power Mussolini was perturbed by German rearmament and designs on Austria. In 1936, however, Mussolini signed the Axis agreement and from that year looked to an eventual German attack on France as a means of seizing Nice, Corsica and Tunisia.

In 1934 Italy began to lay claim to the independent African kingdom of Abyssinia. Britain did her utmost to mediate between the two countries and to get Abyssinia to cede certain territory to Italy. In October 1935 Italy attacked Abyssinia. The Council of the League of Nations condemned Italy as an aggressor and sanctions were applied by over fifty states. These restrictions on exports to Italy were never comprehensive enough and on May 5th 1936 the Italians entered Addis Ababa and occupied the whole of Abyssinia. The Abyssinians had made a courageous stand, but they were no match for aircraft, tanks and poison gas.

When Franco began his revolt against the Spanish Government in July 1936 Italy and Germany gave the rebels support. By the middle of 1937 there were over 40,000 Italian troops in Spain and the Italians and Germans used the Spanish Civil War as an opportunity of experimenting with weapons and strategy. In November 1937 Italy signed the Anti-Comintern (anti-communist) Pact previously concluded between Germany and Japan, and in the following month left the League of Nations. In April 1939 Italy occupied Albania, the Albanian King Ahmed Zog fleeing after a brief resistance. When Germany broke the back of French resistance in 1940, and it was obvious that France would soon be out of the war, Mussolini declared war as an ally of Germany. Hitler allowed him to occupy Nice and Corsica. The next target to Italian ambitions was Greece. By the occupation of Albania across the Adriatic Italy could now mass troops on the northern Epirus border of Greece and, on a variety of pretexts, Italian troops attacked Greece in November 1940. Greek resistance amazed the Italians and it was not until they received the aid of Germany that Greece was finally occupied. Italy entered the war on Germany's side when German victory seemed inevitable. In 1943, however, Italy was the first of the enemy countries to surrender.

JAPAN AND THE FAR EAST

JAPAN, VERSAILLES AND THE WASHINGTON CONFERENCE

Until she was forcibly opened up to western trade in the 'fifties and 'sixties of the last century by the Americans Japan was a backward feudal society. The Japanese soon showed their ability to copy western ways, and by the beginning of this century were being rapidly converted to a modern industrial community. The Japanese began to show that they had military and imperialist ambitions. In 1905 they defeated the Russians and in 1910 annexed Korea. In the First World War Japan joined the Allies and captured the German settlements in China and the various German colonies in the Pacific. Her navy was also used in helping to convoy Allied shipping. Japan went to the Versailles meeting at the end of the war feeling that she deserved treatment as a first-class power.

Japan found at Versailles that, although she was nominally

Japanese Politics

treated as an equal of Britain and America, she was given little opportunity of using the peace treaty to gratify her imperialist ambitions in the Pacific. American and British suspicions of Japan were also increasing, and at the Washington Conference of 1921 Japan found it good policy to agree to limitations of her naval strength and to give guarantees that she had no territorial claims on China. Britain and America thought that by the Washington Conference they had succeeded in obtaining Japanese acquiescence to the *status quo* in the Far East. Japan, however, was merely playing for time. She desired expansion because she wanted to become the dominant Pacific power. In the 'twenties the Japanese population was also increasing at the rate of 900,000 a year. As Japan was not self-supporting, this increase gave an economic impetus to nationalism. The western powers were being very optimistic in thinking the Washington Conference was to have lasting value.

JAPANESE POLITICS

At the close of the First World War Japan had a limited parliamentary government. The vote was only possessed by males having certain property qualifications and there was a great degree of interference in government by the Emperor and the heads of the armed forces. Japan had copied western democratic forms but they had not struck very deeply into her political life. Even the limited democracy that Japan possessed was regarded with hostility by Japanese military circles. The heads of the army and navy regarded any parliamentary control of the armed forces as obnoxious. They desired a thorough totalitarian régime with the Emperor as deified figurehead and real control of the country in their own hands. During the 'twenties and 'thirties the Japanese military caste made no attempt to hide their contempt of the politicians and a totalitarian movement among army officers known as the 'Showa Restoration' attempted a *coup d'état* in February 1936 murdering several liberal statesmen. This outrage was

The Fascist Powers

condemned by the Emperor but attracted a good deal of sympathy from Japanese nationalists. As Japan's imperialist ambitions increased, real control of the country became the prerogative of the militarists. When Japan entered the war in 1941 the country's economic life was organized and directed towards the furtherance of Japanese conquest.

The slogan of Japanese imperialists underlying the history of Japanese aggressions was 'Asia for the Asiatics'. Asia was to be cleared of European colonies and brought under a Japanese 'co-prosperity sphere'. During the 'thirties nationalist propaganda increased and Emperor Hirohito was extolled as the divine head of a chosen people.

JAPAN AND CHINA

Japanese ambitions first turned towards China. In 1911 a revolution in China had overthrown the Manchu dynasty and established a republic. The leader of this revolution was a western educated Chinese called Sun Yat Sen. When the revolution occurred China was a very backward country suffering from internecine warfare between various war lords who controlled the outlying provinces and paid little attention to the central government in Peking. Sun Yat Sen and his Kuomintang movement aimed at unifying and modernizing China. When Sun Yat Sen died in 1925 leadership of the movement eventually passed to his young follower Chiang Kai-shek. Chiang made strenuous efforts to unite the country but the Chinese Communists split with him and formed their own state in the north.[1]

In 1931 the Japanese considered China was ripe for aggression and between September 1931 and January 1932 they occupied the whole of South Manchuria. China appealed to the League of Nations and the Council of the League finally condemned the Japanese action. In February 1932 Japan

[1] Chiang began his career as an enthusiastic supporter of reform but his régime was later to be marked with much corruption which contributed to the seizure of the whole of China by the communists in 1949.

established the puppet state of Manchukuo with the former Chinese ruler Pu Yi as Emperor. Japan now had her eyes on the rest of China and in January 1933 launched an attack across the Manchurian border. The following month Japan resigned from the League of Nations. In July 1937 the Japanese renewed their attack on China—by the end of the month they were in Peking, and Nanking was occupied in August. Free China was soon isolated as a western area with its capital at Chungking under Chiang Kai-shek and the Communist state under Mao Tse Tung.

In 1936 Japan signed the Axis agreement with Germany. In 1941 without declaration of war she suddenly attacked the American naval base at Pearl Harbour. Japan had begun her disastrous attempt at Asiatic domination.

COMMON FACTORS OF FASCISM

After our history of the establishment and aggressions of Fascist régimes in Germany, Italy and Japan we can now attempt to summarize the common factors of Fascism.

1. The first thing we noted was that Germany, Italy and Japan were all countries who wished for revision of the peace settlement at the end of the First World War. Defeated Germany was humiliated by the Treaty of Versailles and the Nazis exploited these nationalist grievances in their rise to power. Italy, although one of the Allies, felt herself to be almost a victim of the treaties and never gained that control of the Adriatic coast which she had expected. At the Washington Conference of 1921 Japan too, found that despite her ambitions she had to acquiesce temporarily in the *status quo* in the Far East. In all these countries movements arose which gave expression to, and stimulated, nationalist sentiment. The Fascist movements were vehemently opposed to the existing territorial dispensation and received support from all who wished for some revision.

2. Fascism came to power in countries where democratic institutions and sentiments were weak. The Weimar régime attempted to introduce overnight a new democratic Republic in a country where democratic sentiment was to prove too weak to maintain it. Italian democracy had been treated in a very cynical fashion by many Italian politicians and in the immediate post-war period failed to maintain that respect for law essential to orderly government. Japanese democracy was always very limited and the Japanese political system essentially authoritarian. In all three countries democracy was also associated with defeat or failure to realize national aspirations. Fascism championed itself as the answer to 'degenerate' democracy.

3. Fascism was largely the product of economic depression and difficulty. In Germany the rise of the Nazis was associated with the worst years of the slump. In Italy and Japan rapidly increasing populations created serious economic difficulty. Fascist movements promised the energetic tackling of these problems.

4. Fascism received the support of all those who feared communism. At the end of the First World War communism was strong in Germany and Italy and potentially strong in Japan. Fascism appeared the only hope to many of combating communism by instituting an authoritarian régime respecting private property.

5. German, Italian and Japanese Fascists shared in varying degrees the common factor of some racialist theory. The Nazis believed in the innate superiority of a so-called Aryan stock formed mainly by the Germans. The racial element was not so prominent in Italian Fascism although Mussolini made much of the supremacy of the ancient Romans and regarded himself as a second Caesar who would bring about Italian domination of the Mediterranean. Japanese Fascism was anti-western—

Asia was to be for the Asiatics and the leaders of the new order the Japanese.

6. Like all totalitarian systems the Fascist régimes of Germany, Italy and Japan were intolerant towards opposition and ruthless in their persecution of anti-Fascist elements. The liberal atmosphere and peaceful disagreements of the democracies seemed to the Fascists weaknesses and the marks of decadence. They failed to appreciate the great strength of democracy which lay behind the apparent disunity.

READING LIST:

Britain and the Dictators, R. W. Seton-Watson (C.U.P.).

Eastern Europe Between the Wars 1918–1941, H. Seton-Watson (C.U.P.).

The Rome-Berlin Axis, E. Wiskemann (O.U.P.).

The Rebuilding of Italy, M. H. H. Macartney (C.U.P.).

The Menacing Rise of Japan, A. Howard and E. Newman (Harrap).

Europe in Decay, L. B. Namier (Macmillan).

Step by Step 1936–1939, W. S. Churchill (Thornton Butterworth).

International Relations Between the Two World Wars 1919–1939, E. H. Carr (Macmillan).

A Short History of International Affairs 1920–1939, G. H. Gathorne-Hardy (Royal Institute of International Affairs).

Chapter Five

BRITAIN AND COMMONWEALTH

When the First World War ended the majority of people in Britain felt very optimistic about the future. Germany, the great pre-war and industrial rival of Britain, was defeated. Most people believed peace was assured for the rest of the century. The League was acclaimed as a brilliant invention that would introduce a period of real co-operation between states. Lloyd George used the phase that Britain would be made into 'A land fit for heroes to live in.' The government had organized the country for victory in a total war and people now expected it to ensure the conditions of progress in the years of peace. In the three years following the war Britain also seemed to enjoy something of a boom in the economic sphere that led many to expect not only a period of peace but also prosperity. There were a number of reasons for this short period of boom which masked the real cost of the war. Firstly was the terrific demand for consumer goods after the shortages of war. This demand created the need for a large labour force and the four million people released from the services were quickly absorbed into jobs and civilian life. Many countries devastated by the war badly needed our goods, and exports began to rise. Resources also did not now have to be used for war purposes and could be devoted to satisfying the needs of consumers. This ephemeral boom concealed the fact that the country was really much poorer because of the colossal cost of the war. Wages in this period rose but by the end of 1921 prices were climbing far more quickly. By the mid-twenties the steep rise in the cost of living led to a growing amount of labour unrest.

The General Strike

THE GENERAL STRIKE

The origins of the General Strike of 1926 are to be found in the depression in the British coal industry of 1925. The history of the British coal industry has always been chequered. Despite the importance of the product and the large labour force employed in the mines—over 600,000 in the inter-war period—little attention was given by governments in the first quarter of the century to labour conditions and the problem of improving efficiency in our mines. From the outbreak of war in 1914 to 1920 the industry was fairly prosperous. In 1921 the industry became depressed, a prosperous period followed again in 1923 and 1924 when the Ruhr mines were not being worked and foreign demands increased, and the industry became depressed again in 1925. Foreign demand slackened, home prices were low and unemployment threatened. In June 1925 the mine owners announced a drastic reduction in wages to cover the loss in profits. The miners' leaders made it clear they were not willing to accept these cuts and threatened strike action. The Prime Minister, Baldwin, appointed an independent Commission to inquire into the dispute under the chairmanship of the Liberal Sir Herbert Samuel. The Samuel Commission made a number of recommendations including measures for the reorganization of the industry. The Commission also considered that some wage reduction was necessary unless the miners were willing to return to the pre-war eight-hour day. The intransigence of both parties made it impossible, however, to implement these recommendations. The owners did not like the suggested reorganization which seemed to introduce a state of semi-nationalization and the miners refused to consider any reduction in wages or increase in the working day—'not a penny off the pay, nor a minute on the day' as their leader A. J. Cook put it. Cook, the leading trades union official of the miners, was a Marxist who had managed to get elected to an important position in the Trades Union Congress, the national body of trades unions. Cook hoped he would be able to exploit the dispute and involve the labour force in other industries in a general strike. The idea of a general strike had always been popular with British socialists since the writings of Robert Owen at the beginning of the nineteenth century. The labour force of the country was to strike *en masse* and this would bring about the downfall of the governing capitalist class without the bloodshed involved in a revolution. Socialists would then assume control of the country and the strikers would all return to work.

On May 1st 1926 the miners stopped work. On May 4th 1926 the T.U.C., under the influence of Cook, ordered all railwaymen, transport workers and printers out in sympathy. The General Strike of 1926 only lasted nine days and proved in the end a fiasco. From the start the strikers never gained the public sympathy which they had hoped for. Most people regarded the General Strike as an attempt to paralyse the economic life of the country against the pleas of the elected government. Volunteers responded to appeals made by Baldwin and helped to keep essential services running, such as the distribution of food. After nine days the workers who had come out on strike in sympathy with the miners returned to work. The miners remained on strike until the autumn but eventually they too had to return to work, agreeing to an additional hour on the working day in order to maintain their wage rates. The General Strike cost the country a lot of money and meant a good deal of hardship to the strikers and their families. Perhaps the only good result of the strike was that it proved a disappointment to the extremists who had hoped it would lead to the overthrow of democratic institutions.

BRITAIN AND IRELAND

When the First World War ended the coalition government of Lloyd George soon found itself faced with civil strife in Ireland that almost amounted to war. The relations of Parliament in London and Ireland had never been particularly happy. From Cromwell's bloody subjugation of the country in the seventeenth century the Irish felt themselves to be an

Britain and Ireland

oppressed race governed finally from London by an indifferent legislature. In the seventies of the last century a strong Irish Nationalist Party appeared whose members advocated varying degrees of home rule. Gladstone became a supporter of the idea of an Irish Parliament for local affairs sitting in Dublin and twice introduced, in 1886 and 1893, Home Rule bills which were both defeated. In 1912 the Liberal government of Asquith decided on granting Ireland a measure of autonomy and introduced a bill for this purpose. The outbreak of war in 1914, however, led to the bill being shelved and its introduction would certainly have meant civil war in Ireland. The bill provided for the control of the whole country by a Dublin Parliament, and the Protestant north-east claimed this would mean their subjugation to the Catholic south. Sir Edward Carson, the leader of the Irish Protestants, actually formed a volunteer army to resist the implementation of home rule if the bill was carried.

In 1916 occurred the tragic Easter Week Rebellion in Dublin. Some Irishmen, disappointed at the failure to obtain home rule, founded an organization known as the Irish Republican Army (I.R.A.). The I.R.A. in Easter Week 1916 thought the time was ripe for a rebellion. The British army was occupied with the war in France and a plot was devized to seize Dublin. The insurrection had some early successes but finally was crushed. Over 450 people were killed in the fighting and fifteen prominent leaders of the rebellion executed afterwards.

In the elections of 1918 seventy-three of the eighty-six Irish seats held by Home Rulers were won by a party called Sinn Fein (Gaelic for 'Ourselves Alone'). The Sinn Fein members refused to sit in the London Parliament and declared the autonomy of Ireland and the foundation of an Irish Parliament in Dublin. The British government refused to accept this *fait accompli* and called on the Royal Irish Constabulary to suppress the Sinn Fein. A bitter war speedily developed with the British authorities finding it increasingly difficult to maintain order in Dublin and southern Ireland. In June 1921 De Valera, the Sinn Fein leader, agreed to a truce. In the talks which followed the truce the Irish were offered dominion status within the Commonwealth. Now the Irish began to disagree among themselves as to whether this offer should be accepted. The moderates finally accepted the offer and although De Valera and the I.R.A. resisted this settlement the new Irish Parliament was in control of all the southern counties by 1923. When war broke out in 1939 southern Ireland remained neutral. Although in 1939 southern Ireland was still theoretically a dominion, many Irish wanted to make it quite clear they had no special connection with Britain. After the war De Valera, who had become Prime Minister, took southern Ireland completely out of the Commonwealth and she is now the Republic of Eire. Since 1921 the six counties of northern Ireland have had their own Parliament in Belfast as well as continuing to send representatives to Westminster.

THE NATIONAL GOVERNMENT

In the general election of 1929 the Labour Party was re-turned as the largest party in the Commons. It did not enjoy a complete majority over both the Conservatives and Liberals but with the promise of Liberal support it was able to take office.[1] The rise of the Labour Party to office had been rapid. The party was founded in 1900 by a group of British socialists who believed that action in the industrial field by Labour through trade unions must also be accompanied by action in the political field. The Labour Party contained many different shades of socialist opinion but all agreed with the principles of democracy and were opposed to Communism. Two of the party's candidates were elected in 1900, twenty-nine in 1906 and forty-two in 1910. During the First World War Labour joined the coalition government and a number of the party leaders served in the Cabinet. The Labour Party was in

[1] The results of the election were Labour 290 seats. Conservative 260 seats. Liberal 60 seats.

The National Government

office for the first time in 1924. It was, however, also in that year a minority government relying on Liberal support and did not last many months. In spite of the fact that it still did not enjoy a complete majority the new Labour Government formed in 1929 was at first optimistic about implementing its programme of expanding social services and beginning the nationalization of certain basic industries such as coal. The cost of the new social security schemes would be met out of higher taxation on large incomes.

Unfortunately, however, for the new government, 1929 was to be the year that the world-wide slump began in America. By the end of the year the effects of this slump were being felt in Britain and unemployment began to rise. Faced with the difficulties created by the slump the Labour Government of Ramsay MacDonald could not concentrate on implementing its programme. By 1931 unemployment reached the staggering figure of three million and it was obvious that crisis measures would be necessary to deal with the situation. It was over the measures necessary to tackle the slump that serious disagreements arose in the Labour Cabinet. Every member of the Cabinet agreed, as one of the economy measures thought necessary, to reductions in the salaries of the civil service, but only MacDonald and a minority were willing to reduce unemployment benefit. MacDonald now turned for support for his economy plans to the Conservatives and Liberals and with the support of Baldwin formed a 'National' Government. MacDonald remained as Prime Minister and enjoyed the support of the Conservatives, the majority of the Liberals and a handful of Labour members. The formation of the National Government caused a serious crisis in the Labour Party. MacDonald and his supporters in the party were expelled, George Lansbury becoming leader of the party. In the general election of 1931, 558 National Government candidates were elected against fifty-six for the Labour opposition. The Labour Party was not to enjoy office again until the formation of the war-time Coalition Government by Churchill in May 1940.

Britain and Commonwealth

The National Government formed in 1931 was to remain in power for nine years and during this period it became increasingly obvious that the government was Conservative in all but name. As a result of National Government economy measures and favourable terms of trade the economic position of the country was improving by 1934. The whole of the cuts in unemployment benefit were restored in that year and half the cuts in the salaries of state employees.

THE BRITISH ECONOMY

We shall in this section of the chapter describe and analyse the main trends and problems of the British economy in the inter-war period. The process known as the 'Industrial Revolution', which we usually place in the period 1750 to 1850, established Britain as the foremost industrial power in the world. A comparatively large labour force, abundant supplies of coal and metals, inventive genius and a powerful navy to protect our shipping, all contributed to this achievement. In the first half of the nineteenth century we were truly the 'workshop of the world'. The manufactures produced by British industry were steadily raising the standard of living at home, and exports of these goods and machinery allowed us to import the food needed for our growing cities and the raw materials required by the factories. By the 'seventies, however, as the following table shows, a number of other countries were forging ahead with their own industrial development.

Cumulative Annual Increase of Manufacturing Production 1873–1913	
U.S.A.	4.8%
GERMANY	3.9%
UNITED KINGDOM	1.8%

The industrial development of other countries meant they did not require so many manufactured imports from Britain as

The British Economy

formerly. In the last quarter of the century, therefore, there began to appear a growing gap between the relative values of British imports and exports. The cost of those imports not covered by exports was paid for by Britain obtaining an abnormal share of the world's shipping, insurance and commercial services. We also drew rich dividends from investments abroad.

The war of 1914 to 1918 forced us to sell many of our overseas investments to pay for the arms we needed. Despite this, the country was still paying its way during the 'twenties. In 1929, however, we were driven to start partially living off this overseas capital. This process continued throughout the 'thirties. The cause of this was that we were no longer selling enough abroad because of foreign industrialization. We also did not attempt energetically enough to increase our export trade in machinery which many countries were buying in large quantities. In 1929 the largest category of our exports was in those commodities expanding least in world trade. The restoration of the Gold Standard in 1925 also proved to be an unfortunate move. Before the First World War the pound was freely convertible at the Bank of England for a stated quantity of gold. During the war we abandoned this close linking of sterling with gold. In 1925 it was thought that a return to the Gold Standard, as the previous system was called, would restore Britain as the great financial centre of the world; foreigners would have increased confidence in our currency if it could be converted into gold. This decision did result in the prestige of sterling being raised for a short period. Unfortunately, however, the return to the Gold Standard affected the prices of our exports and made them more expensive than competitors' products. This became another adverse factor in our balance of payments problem and we were forced to abandon the Gold Standard.

It was fortunate for us in the 'thirties that there was a very favourable movement in the terms of world trade. During the 'thirties the prices of many of our imports fell and at the same time the prices of our exports were maintained. This favourable movement in the terms of trade greatly helped us in our aim of keeping the cashing of overseas investments to a minimum. The cost of the second war of 1939 to 1945 was, however, to make serious inroads into our remaining investments abroad. The post-war period saw Britain facing a difficult balance of payments problem. We shall take up the story of how Britain tackled these economic problems in our last chapter.

THE ABDICATION CRISIS

King George V died in January 1936, eight months after the celebration of his silver jubilee, and was succeeded by his son as Edward VIII. The new king, who was unmarried, soon created an embarassing position for the government by his insistence on marrying an American lady called Mrs Simpson. The government did not consider this lady would be suitable as queen because she was about to obtain in 1936 a divorce for the second time. Baldwin insisted that the King must have the consent of his ministers to any marriage he wished to make and it was their opinion that Mrs Simpson was not acceptable as queen. The King suggested a compromise on the basis of a morganatic marriage. This would have allowed the King to marry Mrs Simpson but would not have given her the status of queen. Such a marriage, however, Baldwin considered, was completely out of keeping with British tradition. The King now had no alternative but to abdicate or end his association with the woman he loved. The King unhesitatingly chose to abdicate and was succeeded by his younger brother George VI.

FOREIGN POLICY BETWEEN THE WARS

British foreign policy in the inter-war years was controlled for nearly the whole period by the Conservatives, the dominant party of the time, and the following factors can be traced in their approach to international relations during this period:

1. The foreign policy of all our governments during this

period was sincerely aimed at the maintenance of peace and the achievement of cordial relations between Britain and foreign powers.

2. From its foundation Britain supported the idea of the League of Nations and hoped that concerted action by the League, e.g. sanctions, would deter any would-be aggressors.

3. During the 'twenties Britain considered France to be suffering from an obsession about Germany and avoided becoming involved in the various French projects for mutual security alliances.

4. Until the invasion of Poland by Hitler in September 1939 Chamberlain hoped to avoid war with Germany by meeting Hitler's territorial demands—the policy which has become known as 'appeasement'. This approach was based on the belief that Hitler did not want a major war but merely desired to amend certain aspects of the territorial settlement at Versailles.

We have already traced in Chapter Four the events eventually leading to the outbreak of war in 1939 and we can here briefly summarize our own mistakes which contributed to its inevitability:

1. In 1919 Britain was far too optimistic in thinking the League would prove to be a partnership of democracies— already there were signs in Italy and Germany that the war did not represent a complete victory over totalitarianism. As early as 1922 Italy, one of the principal members of the Council of the League, was a dictatorship hostile to democratic sentiments and bent on expansion. Our belief that merely moral and economic pressure on recalcitrant countries would maintain peace was also unrealistic. We failed to give the League sufficient 'teeth' to make it an effective organization.

2. Although the excessive reparation demands of France against Germany and her failure to effect an early

rapprochement with the new Weimar Republic were themselves causes of the Nazi rise to power, the repeated warnings of France that German militarism was far from dead should have received more attention from Britain. A strong Anglo-French mutual security pact in the 'twenties, and a careful watch on internal events in Germany, might have done much to deter German militarists.

3. Our policy of attempting to appease Hitler by meeting many of his early demands may also be criticized in that it encouraged him to think we would go to any lengths to avoid war unless actually attacked ourselves.

On September 1st 1939 when Germany attacked Poland, Britain immediately informed Hitler that unless German troops withdrew we should be forced to declare war. Our ultimatum was ignored and, along with France, we declared war. Only twenty years after the 'war to end wars' we were again involved in a life and death struggle to defend ourselves against a serious threat against our way of life.

COMMONWEALTH

The term British Empire, although it is still at times met with has now been replaced by the concept of a British Commonwealth. Empire suggests too much the idea of the domination of one nation over subservient territories and today we prefer to speak of the British Commonwealth of Nations and think of a group of countries, with Britain at the centre, sharing common political ideals and co-operating in the attainment of common goals. The territories comprising the Commonwealth cover a quarter of the land mass of the world with a total population of nearly 600 million. This vast association contains people of different levels of advancement and many different religions and races. It also contains many different types of political organization, but here we may make a broad distinction between completely independent self

Commonwealth

governing countries, or Dominions, and the other territories of the Commonwealth over which there exist varying degrees of control from London.

THE DOMINIONS

Canada, in 1867, was the first territory in the old Empire to attain Dominion status.[1] Australia became a Dominion in 1900, New Zealand in 1907 and South Africa—where we had defeated the Boers only eight years before—in 1910. In 1947 Britain, in keeping with her decision to grant self-government to colonial territories when considered to be ready for it, gave an opportunity to the political leaders in India, Pakistan (the Moslem areas of the India sub-continent), Ceylon and Burma to choose between self-government outside the Commonwealth or as Dominions within it. As a result of the choice made by these countries, India, Pakistan and Ceylon became new British Dominons in January 1948 while Burma chose to leave the Commonwealth and became a Sovereign Republic. By 1948 there were, therefore, seven self-governing Dominions in the Commonwealth—Canada, Australia, New Zealand, South Africa, India, Pakistan and Ceylon. In 1957 the Gold Coast became the independent dominion of Ghana; and there is every indication that Nigeria will attain this status in 1959.

The status of Dominions was defined by the Imperial Conference of Commonwealth Prime Ministers in 1926. Dominions were defined as:

'Autonomous communities within the British Empire, equal in status, in no way subordinate to one another in any aspect of their domestic or external affairs, though united by

[1] Newfoundland was given a measure of self-government as early as 1855 and a few years later had become recognized as a Dominion. Economic difficulties, however, led to the suspension of the Constitution in 1933 and control from London. At the end of the second world war Newfoundland held a plebiscite to decide whether the people wanted restoration of Dominion status, continued control by the British government, or amalgamation with Canada. As a result of this vote Newfoundland joined the Dominion of Canada.

a common allegiance to the crown, and freely associated as members of the British Commonwealth of Nations.'

And the preamble to the Statute of Westminster reads:

'It is in accord with the established constitutional position that no law hereafter made by the Parliament of the United Kingdom shall extend to any of the said Dominions as part of the law of that Dominion otherwise than at the request and with the consent of that Dominion.'

When Britain declared war in 1914 all the Dominions were automatically involved in the struggle. Such was not the case in 1939 although all the Dominions (with the exception of Eire which by 1939 was virtually an independent republic) eventually did join Britain in the struggle. Today the Dominions have their own ambassadors abroad and high commissioners representing their interests in the capital cities of fellow Dominions. They have their own legislative bodies, make their own foreign policy and have their own armed forces. Their common link with other countries of the Commonwealth is quite voluntary.

The British Monarchy still remains an important link uniting the Commonwealth. Although at the beginning of 1954 it appeared likely that Pakistan would join India and also become a Republic with a President as head of state instead of a Governor-General representing the Queen, the Queen is still recognized by India as the symbolic Head of the Commonwealth and will remain an important focus of loyalties. One of the biggest factors in the unity of the Commonwealth is the sharing of common political ideals. In varying degrees all the Dominions have borrowed from the English Constitution when establishing their own system of government and all enjoy some form of representative government. Britain and the Dominions maintain a close liaison with each other. All have representatives in each others capitals and Commonwealth Prime Ministers meet regularly—five such meetings took place between 1946 and 1953. In January 1950 an important meeting of foreign ministers took place in Ceylon and at this meeting a co-operative plan, known as the Colombo Plan, was drawn up for the economic development of South and South East Asia. The British Government contains a minister responsible for the maintenance of good commonwealth relations known as the Secretary of State for Commonwealth Relations. His department, the Commonwealth Relations Office, acts as a clearing house for information of common interest to the Dominions. The Dominions co-operate very closely over economic matters and a Commonwealth Economic Committee maintains a permanent headquarters in London. The Commonwealth also aims at achieving a common defence policy and a good deal of standardization of equipment and weapons has been effected.

THE COLONIES

Although to group all the non-Dominion territories of the Commonwealth under the heading of colonies is not strictly accurate seeing that some of them are termed protectorates and trusteeships, they are all fundamentally similar in not being completely independent. All the non-Dominion territories are controlled to some extent by the British government, or, in the case of a few trusteeships such as Nauru, by a Dominion government. Except for Basutoland, the Bechuanaland Protectorate, Swaziland and the Maldive Islands which are dealt with by the Commonwealth Relations Office, all the Commonwealth territories for which the United Kingdom is responsible are administered through the Colonial Office.

Great differences are to be found in the degree to which individual colonies enjoy control over some of their own affairs. Malta is, for instance, for internal purposes, self-governing, but for defence and foreign relations looks to Britain. The Federation of Rhodesia and Nyasaland, established in 1953, is another self-governing colony; Dominion status has not been granted her because Britain wishes to retain some control over native policy. In some very backward colonies the degree of control

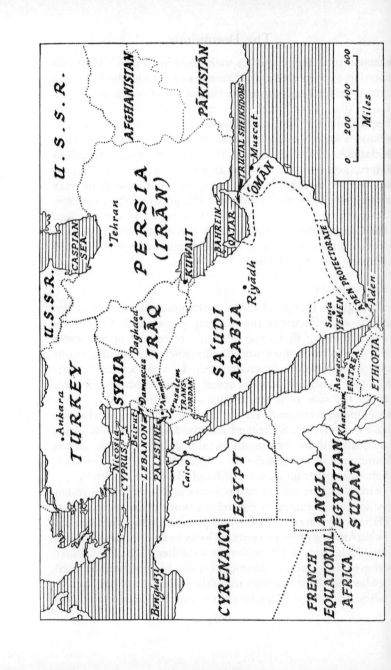

enjoyed by the inhabitants over their territory is very small. It is, however, the cardinal principle of British colonial policy that all our colonies shall be helped to eventually attain some form of self-government.

Since the end of the Second World War Britain has had to meet a great deal of internal trouble in the Colonies of Malaya and Kenya. In Malaya a minority of Communists, armed with weapons supplied to them during the war to fight the Japanese, started a rising aimed at driving out the British. Terrorism became widespread and the position was very serious up to 1953 when the determined policy of the High Commissioner, Sir Gerald Templar, practically eliminated the rebel bands. The Communists failed in Malaya because the majority of the inhabitants, both Malays and Chinese, finally became convinced that their real interests lay in co-operating with the British who were sincere in their desire to lead Malaya towards self-government. In Kenya a large section of an important tribe known as the Kikuyu rose in revolt against Europeans. Their movement became known as Mau Mau and many acts to terrorism were committed by it. By the beginning of 1954 many members of Mau Mau had been rounded up but the situation was still far from being under control.

BRITAIN AND THE MIDDLE EAST

This seems a suitable position to introduce some discussion of British interests in the Middle East. The Middle East is a vital area in world affairs for two reasons. Firstly, because of its rich oil fields in Arabia, Iraq and Iran. Secondly, because of the Suez Canal—Britain's sea link through the Mediterranean with the Far East. Before the First World War the countries of Syria, Lebanon, Israel, Trans-Jordan, Arabia and Iraq were under Turkish control. During the war they were occupied by British troops and their loss to Turkey was confirmed in the Treaty of Lausanne in 1923. Arabia became a completely independent Kingdom. Syria and the Lebanon were placed under French control and Palestine (now Israel),

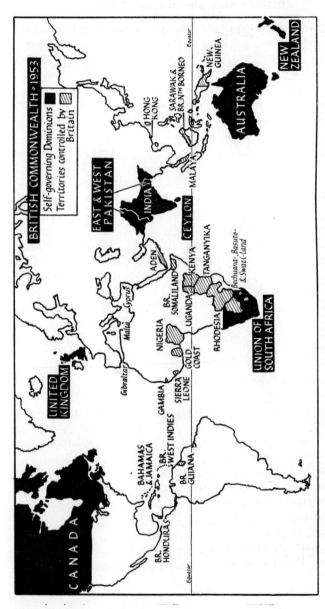

MAP OF COMMONWEALTH 1953 SHOWING SELF-GOVERNING DOMINIONS AND TERRITORIES
CONTROLLED BY BRITAIN

Britain and the Middle East

Trans-Jordan and Iraq became British responsibilities. At the end of the Second World War the Jews in Palestine established the independent state of Israel, and Syria and Lebanon also became independent republics. Britain still retained, however, close connections with Iraq and Trans-Jordan. The Anglo-Iraqi Treaty of Alliance of 1948 also established British bases in Iraq.

Until 1914 Egypt was nominally a province of the Ottoman Empire although her link with Turkey had been very slight since the early nineteenth century. To protect her interests in the Suez Canal Britain occupied Egypt in 1882. The occupation was meant to be only a temporary measure but eventually British troops came to be permanently stationed in Egypt. In 1922 Britain declared Egyptian independence and the Sultan became King Fuad I. Britain retained the right to station troops in Egypt to maintain the security of the Canal. In 1936 the Anglo-Egyptian Treaty was signed which laid down the British right to maintain troops in the Suez Canal zone and the continuation of the Anglo-Egyptian condominium over the Sudan. The Treaty was to last twenty years.

At the end of the Second World War nationalist agitation increased in Egypt for the complete withdrawal of British troops and the unification of the Sudan with Egypt. British troops withdrew to the actual Canal area and a series of negotiations began with the Egyptians aimed at ensuring the adequate defence of the Canal. In July 1952 King Farouk was overthrown and a Republican Government of young army officers came to power. Negotiations were re-opened with the new Premier, Colonel Abdel Nasser. In July 1954 an agreement on the Suez Canal Base was signed in Cairo by Colonel Nasser and Mr. Head, the British Secretary of State for War. This agreement provided for the evacuation of British troops, the maintenance of the base by British and Egyptian technicians, and the return of British troops in case of war in the Middle East. Agreement was also reached on the Sudan. A Sudanese Parliament was established with a view to the

Sudanese eventually choosing whether they wished to join Egypt, become independent, or become a Dominion.

With the evacuation of the Canal Zone our main base in the Middle East became the British colony of Cyprus. It was unfortunate for us that in leaving Egypt for Cyprus we were still not in a position of stationing our troops in territory free from internal trouble and antagonism towards us. Cyprus became British in 1875, after more than 300 years of Turkish rule. British sovereignty over Cyprus was formally recognized by both Turkey and Greece when they signed the Treaty of Lausanne in 1923. Throughout British rule there has been a growing movement for union with Greece, or 'Enosis' as it is called, among the Greek-speaking Cypriots. A complicating factor in the problem of Cyprus was that in 1953 nearly a fifth of the population were of Turkish descent who preferred to remain under British control. By 1953 an extremist wing of the Enosis movement calling itself 'Eoka' was engaging in acts of terrorism against our troops and officials, and also against Cypriots who opposed them. We later found that Eoka was receiving a great deal of help from Archbishop Makarios, the leader of the Greek Orthodox Church on the island. We determined to defeat the terrorists and at the same time try to convince the majority of the Cypriots that they were far better off under the British connexion, and with the possibility of self-government in the Commonwealth, than under the rule of Greece. The British Government was very definite in 1953 that it was unwilling to allow the future of the island to be decided by a plebiscite. A variety of reasons were given for this, including protecting the rights of the Turkish minority and the strategical importance of Cyprus.

READING LIST

Modern Britain 1870–1950, D. C. Somervell (Methuen).

British Politics Since 1900, D. C. Somervell (Dakers).

Britain Between the Wars 1918–1940, C. L. Mowat (Methuen).

Reading List

British Democracy, R. M. Rayner (Longmans).

A Short History of Canada, G. P. de T. Glazebrook (O.U.P.).

The British Commonwealth, Sir W. I. Jennings (Hutchinson).

South Africa, A. Keppel-Jones (Hutchinson).

The British West Indies, W. L. Burn ((Hutchinson).

The Commonwealth and the Nations, N. Mansergh (Roya Institute of International Affairs).

India, Pakistan and the West, P. Spear (O.U.P.).

India, C. H. Philips (Hutchinson).

Young Pakistan, R. M. Khan and H. S. Stark (O.U.P.).

Chapter Six

FRANCE

The end of the First World War left France a shaken and devastated country. Over a million Frenchmen—the cream of her manhood—lay dead. Hundreds of thousands of others had received crippling wounds. A tenth of the country lay in waste including valuable industrial districts. Three hundred thousand houses and 20,000 factories had been destroyed. Two million people were homeless. Although France emerged from the war a victor, her recovery from the four years of suffering was to be slower than that of any other participant. The blood letting and destruction weakened France more than many people in Britain realized. Poor in many natural resources such as coal, and with little modern industrial plant compared with Germany and Britain, France suffered the worst of the fighting in the west during the war. Because of a low birth-rate her population, too, was stationary at just below the 40,000,000 mark and could ill afford the loss of a million potential fathers. That France was reckoned one of the great powers in the inter-war years and, despite the humiliating defeat of 1940, emerged in 1945 to be treated as one of the 'big five' are testimonies to the persistence and courage of the French people.

THE SEARCH FOR SECURITY

The aim of Clemenceau, the French representative at Versailles, was to make Germany realize that aggression does not pay and to ensure that she would not menace France again.

The Search for Security

Clemenceau was old enough to remember the German invasion of France in 1870 and did not wish to see France suffer any more from German attack. Although the Versailles Treaty dealt with Germany in a very harsh way Clemenceau wanted Lloyd George and Wilson to agree to one further provision which he felt essential for the security of Europe—a perpetual French occupation of the left bank of the Rhine. A temporary Allied occupation of the left bank of the Rhine for a period of fifteen years was finally agreed to, but Clemenceau remained adamant that this did not go far enough.

France was the least optimistic of the Allies about the possibilities of maintaining peace. The First World War had nearly been won by Germany, and Germany, many Frenchmen thought, would one day desire vengeance for the humiliating Versailles Treaty which did not go far enough in ensuring she would not endanger peace again. Throughout the 'twenties, when Britain was very optimistic about international relations, few Frenchmen lost their fear of Germany. Professor Carr has written:

'The most important and persistent single factor in European affairs following 1919 was the French demand for security.'[1]

In the inter-war period French governments sought unremittingly for means of ensuring the safety of France against potential new German dangers.

In 1921 the French Prime Minister was an outstanding statesman called Briand. Briand, like the majority of Frenchmen, was perturbed about a possible resurgence of German power, but did sincerely hope that good relations would be achieved with the new Weimar régime and that eventually the scars and bitterness of war would heal. Briand felt that his task was to work for better relations with Germany, while at the same time seeking guarantees from Britain that aid would

[1] *International Relations Between the Two World Wars 1919–1939.* Chapter I. 'France and her Allies'. Macmillan, 1947.

always be available for France if she were attacked. Shortly after coming into office Briand attended a conference of Allied statesmen at Cannes. At this meeting Briand aimed at extracting a definite guarantee from Lloyd George that Britain would immediately help France if she suffered aggression. Britain, however, not only wanted to avoid becoming involved in a French system of alliances, but also considered France's obsession about her security to be unnecessary with defeated Germany being so weak. Briand failed to get his guarantee.

Although the Cannes meeting proved a disappointment Briand was conspicuously successful in ranging a number of minor European powers alongside France in a mutual security system. In 1921 France concluded a mutual security pact with the new state of Poland. In terms of population, resources and territory Poland was potentially an important east European state, and France might have seen in Poland a substitute in the old pre-war alliance with Tsarist Russia. Shortly after concluding this agreement with Poland, France formed an alliance with the three countries known as the Little Entente— Czechoslovakia, Yugoslavia and Rumania. These countries were all beneficiaries of the peace treaties, largely at the expense of Hungary, and had grouped together to prevent Hungarian revision of the settlement. By her agreement with Poland and the Little Entente France began to feel she was surrounding Germany with her allies.

Briand was succeeded as Premier shortly after the failure of the Cannes meeting by the rabid anti-German Poincaré. It was Poincaré who shortly after becoming Prime Minister ordered the French occupation of the Ruhr because of Germany defaulting with reparation payments. Poincaré was in office until the 1924 election and became Prime Minister again in 1926, resigning because of ill-health in 1929. During his term of office Poincaré did his utmost to strengthen France's position. Close relations were maintained with Poland and the Little Entente countries. Poincaré, like Briand, also tried to obtain a

The Search for Security

definite guarantee from Britain. He almost succeeded in achieving this, but when he demanded concrete details of the extent of British military aid in case of German attack the discussions broke down. Poincaré's Minister for War during the period 1926 to 1929 was Maginot who, under Poincaré's inspiration, began the construction of the ill-fated Maginot Line. The idea of the Maginot Line was that it would cover all French territory liable to German attack. The Line, finally, however, only stretched from the Swiss to the Belgian frontier and the Germans in 1940 were able to penetrate France through Belgium.

In 1934 a Conservative, Doumergue, became Prime Minister who appointed Barthou as his Foreign Minister. By 1934 the Nazis were firmly in power in Germany and Barthou set himself the task of building up under French leadership a great anti-Nazi bloc which he hoped would eventually include Russia and even Fascist Italy. Before he could put these schemes into operation, however, Barthou was assassinated by a Croat fanatic in Marseilles along with King Alexander of Yugoslavia who was paying a state visit to France. Laval, who was later to play a notorious rôle in the Vichy régime, succeeded Barthou. Laval at first tried to improve relations with Germany and when these overtures failed began to look to Italy as a possible ally. To ingratiate himself with Mussolini Laval only half-heartedly supported sanctions against Italy when she attacked Abyssinia. Laval's vacillating policy soon made him unpopular and he fell from power in 1935. In the general election of 1936 a left wing group of parties known as Le Front Populaire under the leadership of the socialist Blum came to power. Blum's government was opposed to the continual appeasement of Germany and also wanted to aid the Spanish Republicans in their fight against Franco. In 1938 Blum was succeeded by the conservative Daladier. Daladier took part in the Munich agreement and his government declared war on Germany after the attack on Poland.

France

France's search for security against Germany was not aided by the chronic instability of French Governments during this period. In Britain once a party has been elected to power the public can usually assume that it will be in office for a reasonable time even if it does not stay in office right up to its maximum life of five years. Between 1919 and 1939 the average life of governments in this country was over three years. In France for the same period it was only ten months, there being more changes in government in France, for instance, between 1930 and 1936 than there were in Britain between 1900 and 1940. What reasons were there for this chronic instability?

The biggest factor in this instability was the existence of a great variety of political parties, a 'powder of parties' as it has been called. None of these parties was strong enough to form a government on its own and this made various combinations necessary which, once office was achieved, almost inevitably soon dissolved in argument. In Britain we have two major parties and it is rarely that one of these cannot form a government on its own after an election: the British two-party system tends to favour stable government.

Another important factor was the strength of the second chamber—the Senate—in the French political system. In Britain we have a two-chamber system of government but the upper house, the Lords, are very inferior in power to the Commons and cannot overthrow a party in power in the Commons. In France this was not the case. The Chamber of Deputies (the equivalent of our House of Commons) was elected by manhood suffrage every four years. The Senate was elected by a complicated system from the local authorities, with a bias in representation for the rural areas, and possessed equal legislative power with the Deputies. Senators served for nine years, one third retiring each year. They had to be at least forty years of age. Elected at different times to the Deputies and thus often having opposition parties in majority, and tending to represent very conservative forces, the Senate often brought about the downfall of a government by holding up legislation even when this had been passed by the Deputies. We have already noted (in Chapter Three) that the difficulties created by the election at different times of the two legislative bodies in France are also to be found in the American system of government.

In the Chamber of Deputies there was also at any one time a great number of ex-ministers conspiring to bring down the government in power and achieve office again. This meant there never appeared to the ordinary member a shortage of possible substitutes for the existing ministers. Groups of opposition parties coming together to bring down a government also realized that the collapse of the parties in power did not necessarily involve a new election—by bringing down the government they were not thereby placing their own membership of the Deputies in danger.

When the new constitution of the Fourth Republic was being devized after the end of the war in 1945 great stress was laid on attempting to learn from the defects of the Third Republic and ensuring France would enjoy stable government in the future. Since 1945, however, and mainly because of the multiplicity of political parties, France has still been cursed by the instability and ephemeral character of her governments.[1]

ANTI-REPUBLICAN FORCES

In Britain few people have ever been opposed to the system of political democracy under which we live. Even during the nineteen thirties when the British Fascist Movement of Mosley and the Communists were making determined efforts to swell their ranks by noisy campaigning our constitutional government did not seem seriously threatened from within. In France,

[1] This was particularly marked in 1954 when France badly needed a stable régime to negotiate at the Geneva Conference to bring to an end the Indo-Chinese war.

however, in the inter-war years this was not the case. A large influential section of politically alive Frenchmen were vehemently opposed to the Third Republic and to any system of democracy. Not only were the various French Governments of this period having to occupy themselves with the German danger from without—they were also very concerned about the strength of anti-democratic forces within the Republic.

Chief among these movements wishing to bring about the fall of the Third Republic, and the substitution of some form of totalitarian state, was the Action Française. Although rarely represented in the French Parliament, the Action Française was an influential and vociferous force in French politics throughout the inter-war years. It owned a newspaper with a large circulation named after the party and contained among its members some of the recognized intellectual leaders of the day. Chief among these were the classical scholar Charles Maurras and the writer Leon Daudet. The party made a particular appeal to Communist-obsessed members of the middle class and to those social failures who felt themselves a cut above the members of the various left-wing parties. Maurras regarded the French Revolution of 1789 as a disaster for France, and wished to return to an authoritarian society based on a union between the Catholic Church and Monarchy. The party was the only remaining influential royalist body in France, and its youth movement—whose chief occupation was indulging in street brawls with Jews and socialists—was actually called the Servants of the King.[1]

Another anti-democratic movement very active in the 'thirties was Colonel de la Rocque's Croix de Feu. The Croix de Feu was a movement of ex-servicemen who wished to substutute some form of military dictatorship for the Third Republic. The Croix de Feu was similar to the Action

[1] The Action Française was in a peculiar position throughout its later history because of having been disowned by both the Catholic Church and the French Orleanist Pretender.

Française in being anti-democratic but there were a number of important differences between the two movements. The Croix de Feu was not a royalist movement and preferred some form of state along Fascist lines. De la Rocque was very much influenced by Mussolini's seizure of power in 1922, and no doubt hoped his movement would eventually be strong enough to repeat the march on Rome by a march on Paris. The Croix de Feu also did not look back nostalgically to the ancient régime as the golden age for France: its members were not sentimental traditionalists. Despite these differences, however, these two movements and various other pseudo-fascist groups could often combine to embarrass and harass the Third Republic. An opportunity seemed to present itself for this when the Stavisky scandal broke out in 1934.

Stavisky was a Russian swindler, long resident in France, who committed suicide in January 1934 to avoid arrest. During the weeks following the suicide the maximum amount of political capital was made out of the case by the various anti-Republican groups. The Action Française claimed the Prime Minister Chautemps and other leading politicians were implicated in Stavisky's rackets. The Stavisky case, Maurras claimed, showed the corruption underlying the Third Republic. On the 6th February, riots engineered by the Croix de Feu broke out in front of the Chamber of Deputies. On the 9th February the Communists —the authoritarian party of the left—also staged demonstrations. The violence of these incidents convinced many Frenchmen that the Third Republic was seriously threatened. In 1936 Blum, the leader of the Socialist Party, was elected to office and an important part of his programme aimed at destroying the para-military forces of the totalitarian parties. Blum abolished the uniformed youth movement of the Action Française and passed legislation restricting the activities of the Croix de Feu. The Third Republic had realized that the toleration by a democracy of those internal forces aimed at its destruction can be carried to extremes.

France

On the 3rd September 1939 France declared war on Germany
—Germany had invaded Poland and refused to withdraw her
forces. Britain also declared war alongside France and the two
Allies settled down to building up their military strength for a
future assault in Germany. In June 1940, however, Germany
struck first. Her armies quickly occupied Holland and Belgium
and struck towards Paris, taking the Maginot Line in the rear.
France collapsed in the space of a few weeks, the British forces
only being saved by the miracle of Dunkirk. Many Frenchmen
were opposed to surrender. Daladier wished to continue the
fight from the French colonies and Churchill suggested a
federation of the two countries. A brilliant French soldier
General de Gaulle fled to England and there raised Free
French forces to continue the fight.

Meanwhile, in France, a peace treaty was signed with the
Germans by the aged Marshal Pétain who had formed a new
government at Vichy. This treaty gave Germany the northern
areas of France including Paris, and also allowed her to
occupy the whole area of the French Atlantic coast. Pétain
announced that the defeat was due to the lack of discipline in
the Third Republic and that French recovery lay through a
more ascetic existence. An influential member of Pétain's
government was Laval whom we will remember was Foreign
Minister in 1934. Round Pétain also gathered all those anti-
democratic elements who had worked for the destruction of the
Third Republic. Resistance to the Germans in France continued in the form of a strong underground movement, and
when Allied forces landed in France in 1944 General de
Gaulle's Government returned with them. The collaborators
of Vichy were eventually tried. Pétain, Maurras and others
received long prison sentences. Laval and de Brinon
(the Vichy representative in Paris during the German
occupation) were shot. The Fourth Republic had been
born.

Reading List

READING LIST

Democracy in France, D. Thomson, (Royal Institute of International Affairs).

The French Political Scene, D. M. Pickles (Nelson).

Why France Fell, A. Maurois (Lane).

The Last Days of Paris, A. Werth (Hamilton).

Chapter Seven

THE SECOND WORLD WAR
1939-1945

It is obviously not possible in a book of this size to enter into any very detailed account of the course of the Second World War of 1939 to 1945. In this chapter we shall attempt to cover the most significant events of these six momentous years. The war eventually became a world struggle between the democracies and the Soviet Union on the one hand, and the Fascist states of Germany, Italy and Japan on the other.

The aggressive policy of the Fascist powers was bound finally to lead them into conflict with the democracies. The period 1939 to 1942 (Japan entered the war in 1941) saw the aggressors reach the height of their success. At the end of 1942 Germany had under occupation France, Belgium, Holland, Luxembourg, Norway, Denmark, Czechoslovakia, the Baltic states, Yugoslavia, Poland, Greece, Austria and great slice of European Russia where her armies had occupied the Ukraine, surrounded Leningrad and were a threat to Moscow and the Caucasus. Axis forces were still in North Africa. Germany had at this time as allies, Italy, Finland, Hungary, Bulgaria and Rumania, and had not despaired of involving Spain in the war with the promise of Gibraltar as a reward. Japan was also at the zenith of her fortunes during 1942. By the end of that year, besides her earlier conquests in China, she had driven into Indo-China, Malaya, the Dutch East Indies, Siam and Burma, and was a real threat to India. From 1943, however, we can trace the decline of the Axis powers. After a crushing defeat at Stalingrad in January 1943 German fortunes in

The Second World War 1939–1945

Russia sank rapidly until by the end of 1944 Russian armies were on German soil. Italy capitulated to the Allies in 1943 and after this Germany occupied the north of the country establishing Mussolini as the puppet dictator of a Fascist Republic. Meanwhile, the Allied bombing offensive against Germany was steadily mounting in force, and during the period from early 1943 to April 1945 Germany's industrial centres were reduced to rubble. As the inevitability of her eventual defeat became more obvious Germany found it increasingly difficult to maintain her hold on the occupied territories where her policy of exploitation and brutality had built up large resistance movements. In 1943 Japan still appeared to be in a powerful position, but a rapid build-up of American and Allied strength in the Pacific was soon to be unleashed upon her—during the following year Allied forces fought their way back into Burma and many of the scattered Pacific islands occupied by Japan. Germany surrendered in May 1945— Hitler and Goebbels dying in the ruins of Berlin and other Nazi leaders being captured and placed on trial for war crimes at Nuremburg. Mussolini was executed by Italian partisans. Japan held on for three more months but the dropping of atom bombs on Nagasaki and Hiroshima put her also out of the war.

'THE PHONEY WAR'

The invasion of Poland on the 1st September 1939 was followed two days later by a declaration of war against Germany by Britain and France. We warned Germany that unless her forces were withdrawn we should be forced to take this step. Germany ignored our demands and war became inevitable. The Poles resisted the German attack to the best of their ability, but the invasion of her eastern territory by Russia administered the *coup de grâce*. In a month her territory had been occupied and divided between Germany and Russia. We declared war on Germany because of her invasion of Poland. Should we now declare war on Russia for her aggression?

The Second World War 1939–1945

We did not take this step and later events were to show how wise we were.

The period September 1939 to May 1940 has gone down in histories of these years as the 'phoney war' period. A great deal did in fact happen during these months, as we shall shortly show, but certainly on the western front all was quiet. French and British strategy at this time rested on the idea that their strength should be steadily built up for an eventual assault on the German positions. It was thought that if the Germans attacked first they could be easily held by the Maginot Line. The Maginot Line, however, only stretched to the Belgian frontier and the Germans were later to show of what little value it was.

When the war started Britain feared she would almost immediately become the objective of heavy air attack. Memories of the blitz bombings of Spanish Civil War days were probably responsible for these fears. A mass evacuation of children from our industrial centres took place in September and October 1939, although heavy air-raids were not to come for over a year. Most of these evacuees eventually drifted back home and had to be re-evacuated in 1940. Britain soon took on all the dismal sign of a country beginning a total war—some foods became scarce and rationing of essentials was introduced in January 1940, gas-masks were issued, air-raid shelters were dug, and a Civil Defence force formed. Taxation also rose to a level the country had not known before. Income tax, for instance, was to reach ten shillings in the pound, as against the four shillings in the pound of 1939. The country was cheered during these dismal events by the way in which the Dominions rallied round us. Canada, Australia and New Zealand immediately declared war on Germany when they knew we had taken this step. South Africa was soon to follow, and General Smuts became Prime Minister of a government determined to prosecute the war with every effort. Eire remained neutral, but many Irish citizens volunteered to help us.

At the beginning of the First World War Germany had a

formidable navy. In 1939 she possessed only few surface craft, and in December 1939 lost one of the largest of her battleships when the *Graf Spee* was scuttled off Uruguay after she had been heroically chased by three small British cruisers called the *Ajax*, *Achilles* and *Exeter*. The main German threat at sea was to be the submarine and when the war began the Germans stepped up their production of these. In the first winter of the war, however, they placed most reliance upon their magnetic mines and hoped these would inflict crippling losses among Allied shipping. Fortunately for us, one of these mines was washed up intact. The weapon was analysed and 'degaussing' girdles for ships invented. These girdles for iron or steel ships were designed to neutralize the magnetic fields of the German mines and proved a very effective protection against them.

In April 1940 the Germans without warning suddenly attacked Norway. In a few days they occupied the capital Oslo and the southern part of the country. During the previous winter the Norwegians had done their utmost to remain on good terms with the Germans, even allowing German war-ships the shelter of Norwegian territorial waters. On one occasion the German cruiser *Altmark* was carrying British prisoners to Germany through these waters. The British cruiser *Cossack* entered the fjord where the *Altmark* was sheltering. The German ship was boarded and the prisoners released. The Norwegians protested about our action but prob-ably realized they had no case. The German attack on her demonstrated the futility of attempting to appease Hitler. We established a force in the far north of Norway at Narvik and hoped to hold at least a small part of the country. The Germans, however, eventually attacked Narvik and we were forced to evacuate the whole of Norway.

The rapid German successes in Norway, and our failure to effectively meet this attack, were to bring about the fall of the Chamberlain Government. On the 8th and 9th May 1940, the government was heavily criticized in the Commons by both Labour and Conservative members of Parliament. On the 10th May Chamberlain resigned and Winston Churchill became Prime Minister of a Coalition Government bent on pursuing the war with vigour until final victory. Important posts in the cabinet were given to the leaders of the Labour Party, Clement Attlee becoming Deputy Prime Minister. Some Liberals were also included. This Coalition Government headed by Churchill was to remain in office until the defeat of Germany in 1945.

THE DEFEAT OF FRANCE

The day Churchill became Prime Minister was also the day on which the Germans launched their great offensive in the west. The Germans did not strike at the Maginot Line, as we had rather optimistically hoped, but drove through Holland and Belgium and into France north west of the Maginot Line. The Dutch army surrendered in four days and the Belgians in seventeen. The German break-through in the Ardennes rolled back the British army under Lord Gort, and a large part of the French army, to the Dunkirk beaches east of the straits of Dover. By the end of May it appeared as if the British army was doomed to total destruction or surrender. Hitler already began to boast that Dunkirk was virtually a huge prison camp. The Dunkirk 'miracle', however, was about to happen. The Royal Navy assembled a mixed collection of nearly nine hundred vessels, ranging from small privately manned cabin-cruisers to her largest battleships. In perfect weather this fleet sailed across the channel to rescue our forces. It now became a race between our ships crossing and re-crossing the channel and the Germans, who were rapidly advancing to the coast. Meanwhile, the Luftwaffe did its utmost to hinder the evacuation. Constant low level strafing attacks were made on our ships and on the long lines of troops waiting patiently on shore. The Royal Air Force did its utmost to meet this challenge and shot down 179 German aircraft over Dunkirk for the loss of only twenty-nine of their own. By the time the Germans reached Dunkirk, over 355,000 of

The Defeat of France

our troops (nine tenths of our forces in France) had been rescued and we had won the race. The Germans felt angry and cheated, although they had the consolation of capturing large quantities of equipment which we had not been able to destroy.

After the evacuation of our forces France struggled on alone for a few more weeks against the Germans. Churchill, realizing that resistance to the Germans in France was near its end, advised the French Government to go to French North Africa and carry on the struggle there. Defeatism was now rampant in France and the advice was ignored. On the 22nd June Italy declared war on France and Britain. At the end of the month a new French Government under Marshal Pétain surrendered to the Germans and Italians. The terms dictated by the Germans were harsh—half of France, including Paris and the Atlantic coastline, was to be occupied. The Germans promised they would not use the French fleet if it was immobilized. We placed no trust in these guarantees to the French and thought it advisable to take over those parts of the French fleet in home ports. We were also forced to bombard the French ships at Oran in Morocco to prevent their escape. Not all Frenchmen were willing to agree that the war was over and total victory had been won by the Germans. A substantial part of the French forces in Britain rallied to a 'Free French' movement headed by General de Gaulle. Important parts of the French Empire, including Equatorial Africa, also announced their determination to carry on the fight.

The great question now was, would Germany attempt an invasion of Britain? Although we managed to evacuate most of our army from Dunkirk, nearly all its equipment had been sacrificed. After their lightning victories in France it is probable that the Germans also considered our morale would be very low. Everything pointed to them attempting to destroy us and thus gain a total victory in the west. One essential had to be satisfied, the Germans realized, before any invasion could succeed. That essential was the destruction of the Royal

Air Force. With no opposition in the air the Germans could carry large numbers of their troops across the channel by air in transport aircraft. The bombers of the Luftwaffe could also sink any of our battleships impeding the sea crossing by German shipping packed with troops.

The attempt of the Luftwaffe, between the second week of August and early October 1940, to destroy the Royal Air Force has gone down to history as the 'Battle of Britain'. The Battle of Britain justly ranks as one of the most important battles ever fought in the history of war. If the Luftwaffe had been the victor Hitler would almost certainly have carried through his invasion project, and without air opposition may well have got enough of his troops across the channel to subdue us. The Battle of Britain proved to be a crushing defeat for the Luftwaffe—the first defeat suffered by the German air force since the beginning of the war. The Germans planned to destroy our aircraft in two ways. Firstly, they aimed to raid and heavily bomb our airfields with a view to destroying many of our aircraft on the ground and making it impossible for the others to take off. Secondly, they determined to raid our channel ports hoping this would draw many of our aircraft to defend our shipping. The Luftwaffe considered it could then shoot down these aircraft. The Luftwaffe, however, had greatly underestimated the quality of aircraft such as the Spitfire and Hurricane, and also the dash and ability of our pilots. By the end of the battle 1,733 German aircraft had been shot down and the Royal Air Force had scored a great victory. The Germans abandoned any immediate plan to invade us and the Luftwaffe discontinued its daylight attacks on Britain.

After their failure to destroy the Royal Air Force in August and September 1940, the Germans began a policy of night bombing aimed at crippling our centres of production and lowering civilian morale. These attacks lasted right through the second winter of the war and only eventually tailed off after the German invasion of Russia in the summer of 1941. This bombing did much damage to our main cities, particu-

The Defeat of France

larly to London, and killed over 60,000 civilians and wounded many thousands more. Despite this new attempt to convince us the war was lost Britain stood firm. For twelve months after the surrender of France, Britain faced the might of Germany alone.

VICTORY IN AFRICA

It was fortunate for us that events in Africa were so cheering during the months we fought alone. When Italy declared war her forces in East Africa forced us to evacuate the unimportant colony of British Somaliland. The African empire of Italy was, however, doomed. We were soon to make the Italians bitterly regret their entry into the war. In the winter of 1940 to 1941 occurred General Wavell's Libyan campaign. At this critical point of the war we sent to Egypt for Wavell's use some heavy Matilda tanks and substantial equipment. Wavell determined to use these supplies to the full. The Italian forces in Libya were far superior in numbers to our troops in Egypt. Thinking an easy victory was in their grasp the Italians advanced to Sidi Barrani some fifty miles within Egyptian territory. There they rested and prepared for a triumphal march to Cairo. Wavell quickly struck, and nipping off the Italians took over 40,000 prisoners. In a few weeks we were in Benghazi, 300 miles from our starting point, and General Graziani's army was destroyed.

During the same period Italian East Africa was successfully mopped up. The victories here were gained by the two Indian divisions of General Platt in the Sudan, and the mixed African troops of General Cunningham in Kenya. In January 1941 Platt struck into Eritrea and—after a stiff battle at Keren—pushed through to the Red Sea by April. In the same month Cunningham's army advanced into Somaliland and, covering the fantastic distance of 1,700 miles in fifty-seven days, reached the Abyssinian capital of Addis Ababa in April.

Their heavy defeats in Africa so soon after entering the war greatly dispirited the Italians. They were also to experience nothing but disaster at sea. At the battle of Cape Matapan the Italian navy was badly mauled by a naval force under Admiral Cunningham. It was only German intervention that was to save the Italians from utter humiliation also in Greece. After their easy victory over France the Italians attacked Greece from their Adriatic colony of Albania. On paper the Italians had an overwhelming superiority and expected the war to be over in a few weeks. The Greeks, however, fiercely resisted and actually managed to drive the invaders back into Albania. Fortunately for the Italians help from their German allies was shortly to be available for in the spring of 1941 Germany achieved domination over central Europe and the Balkans. Hungary, Roumania and Bulgaria became her allies and Yugoslavia was defeated and occupied. From Yugoslavia German forces struck into Greece. We did everything we possibly could to help the Greeks and sent an army from North Africa to her aid. These forces we finally had to evacuate to the island of Crete which we decided to try and hold. In May 1941 the Germans invaded with strong paratroop forces, and because our airfields had been heavily bombed and were untenable, we were not able to offer effective resistance. In two weeks Germany had occupied the whole of Crete.

In April 1941 a pro-Axis Iraqi politician called Raschid Ali seized power in Baghdad. We had no intention of allowing Iraq to fall under German control and quickly ousted Raschid Ali who had to flee. We also feared that Germany might attempt to establish a foothold in Vichy-controlled Syria. In June 1941, therefore, a mixed British-Free French force entered Syria and occupied the country.

During the second winter of the war the Germans made a determined effort with their submarines to starve Britain into surrender. Our shipping losses at first were heavy but by the use of convoys and detective apparatus we slowly began to win the battle. By the last winter of the war our methods of detecting and destroying submarines had advanced to the

point where submarines were becoming only of nuisance value
and few of those leaving German ports were returning.

HITLER ATTACKS RUSSIA

In the spring of 1941 Germany began to build up large forces
in Poland and East Prussia. Hitler always described Russia as
being the first enemy of Germany and emphasized that German
colonization was to be sought in the east. We warned Russia
that our intelligence reports suggested an assault on her was
impending. Stalin, however, did not treat these warnings with
the seriousness which they deserved. When German forces
attacked in June the Russians were far from prepared for them.
Many western military observers did not consider Russian
resistance would last for long. With the oil and grain of Russia,
Germany would also be in a powerful position to prosecute the
war against us.

The German plan was to trap and annihilate the Red army
and seize the main industrial and agricultural areas of
European Russia. Their campaign began with some startling
successes. The Germans took hundreds of thousands of
prisoners and by November 1941 their forces had surrounded
Leningrad, were only fifty miles from Moscow and had
reached the mouth of the Don. Despite these successes the
Germans failed to achieve their objective of destroying all
Russian resistance before the onset of winter. Large areas of
Russia were occupied but opposition to the German advance
was stiffening and new Russian armies were being trained
behind the front by General Budyenny. At Christmas the
Germans made a concentrated effort to take Moscow. The
assault failed and the Germans were forced to realize that
complete victory over Russia would not be won easily.

When Germany attacked Russia, Churchill immediately
declared that every aid would be given to the Russians
despite the fact that he, and the majority of Britons, loathed
communism. The enemy, Churchill declared, is Nazism, and
whoever fights Nazism must be assisted. From the summer of

1941 to the end of the war we sent large quantities of equipment to the Russians. Most of this equipment was carried either by ship to the north Russian ports of Murmansk and Archangel or overland via Persia to the Caucasus.

Britain itself also received a great deal of aid during 1941 from America. In January 1941 Congress passed the Lease-Lend Act which virtually gave Roosevelt the power to afford every aid to Britain short of declaring war. In August 1941 Churchill and Roosevelt met on a battleship in the Atlantic and promulgated the 'Atlantic Charter' setting out their common ideals and objectives. Even before she entered the war in December 1941, America was described as the 'arsenal of democracy'.

During 1941 we steadily increased our bombing of German industrial centres. As the following table shows the weight of bombs dropped on Germany rose steeply throughout the war:

Tonnage of Bombs Dropped on Germany	
Year	*Tons of Bombs Dropped*
1940	7,000
1942	37,000
1944	273,000

This heavy bombing—in which the Americans were later to participate—devastated large areas of Germany and seriously affected German morale. The Germans showed amazing ingenuity in trying to keep transport services and production going despite this bombing. They were, however, unable to overcome the heavy saturation bombing of the later months of the war.

JAPANESE AGGRESSION

On the 7th December 1941, Japanese bombers attacked and paralysed the United States Pacific Fleet lying in Pearl Harbour, Hawaii. The attack was made while Japanese delegates were

U.S.S.R.　　　U.S.S.R.

MONGOLIA　　MANCHURIA

Vladivostok

Peking

CHINA

KOREA

JAPAN

Tokyo

Yokohama to
Pearl Harbour
3380 miles

Nanking　Nagasaki

Yangtze Kiang　Shanghai

Hiroshima

INDIA

Okinawa　　Iwojima

Canton　FORMOSA

Pacific

BURMA

F. INDO CHINA

Hong Kong

Rangoon

THAILAND

Manila

PHILIPPINE

ISLANDS

Guam

MALAY
STATES

Palau　Yap

SUMATRA

Singapore BORNEO

Ocean

EQUATOR

Batavia　CELEBES

NEW
GUINEA

JAVA

Darwin

Port
Moresby

Coral
Sea

The
FAR EAST
(Mercator's Projection)
Nautical Miles · Equatorial Scale
0　200　400　600

AUSTRALIA

THE AREA OF JAPANESE AGGRESSION

actually having talks in Washington with the American Government on the maintenance of peace. Shortly after the Japanese aggression Germany and Italy also declared war on America. By the beginning of 1942 America was, therefore, at war with all the Axis powers. Because we wanted the Russians to concentrate on the struggle with Germany, we were relieved when Japan made no attack on Siberia. In the closing weeks of the war when Germany had surrendered, Russia struck into Manchuria and quickly overcame Japanese forces there.

During the six months following their bombing of Pearl Harbour the Japanese achieved a number of spectacular successes. Between December 1941 and April 1942 their armies overran Burma, Malaya, Singapore, the Philippines and Java, and were also threatening India and Australia.

In May 1942, a beginning was made in halting the fantastic advance of the Japanese. The naval battles of the Coral Sea and Midway Island convinced them that they had not achieved naval dominance in the Pacific. The Australians also held firm in the mountains of New Guinea. The Japanese regarded New Guinea as a stepping stone to Australia and were bitterly disappointed at their failure to take the southern part of the island.

THE BEGINNING OF THE END

By the autumn of 1942 the Axis powers were at their zenith. From this point we can trace their decline. Firstly, let us look at events in North Africa, for the winter of 1942–1943 was to bring about the complete elimination of the Axis in Africa. In 1942 the Germans sent to Libya an army trained for desert warfare called the Afrika Korps. This army was commanded by the very able General Rommel. The German intention was that Rommel would bolster the Italians and eventually strike into Egypt and capture the Suez Canal. In September 1942 the Germans advanced into Egypt and got to within fifty miles of Alexandria. Our commander-in-chief in the Middle East

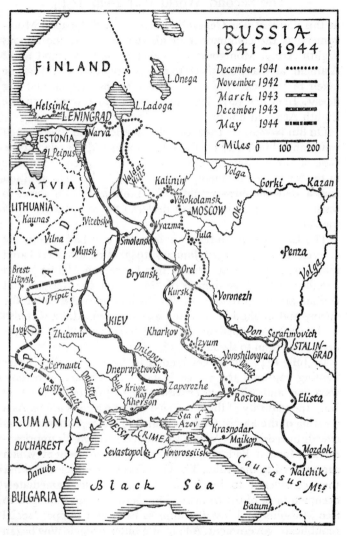

THE FRONT LINE IN RUSSIA: DECEMBER 1941—MAY 1944

at this moment was General Alexander, with General Montgomery as the commander of his striking force, the famous Eighth Army. Montgomery decided to make a stand at El Alamein, an excellent place to choose because it could not be taken in the rear. Here the Afrika Korps met its first big defeat. In a few days Rommel was in full retreat with the Eighth Army in hot pursuit.

On 8th November 1942, British, American and Free French units landed in Vichy controlled Morocco and Algeria. At the time of our landings Admiral Darlan, an important minister in the Vichy Government, was in North Africa. The position was a delicate one—would Darlan order French forces to resist us? Fortunately, Darlan declared for co-operation with the Allies.

The Eighth Army advancing from the east had meanwhile entered Tripoli on 23rd January 1943. Axis forces retreated into Tunisia where our armies from Libya and Algeria joined together. After three months of stiff fighting the German and Italian armies surrendered. We had cleared Africa of the enemy and in Tunisia captured 250,000 men. Malta was also no longer surrounded by Axis-held territory and air attacks upon her began to slacken.

In July 1943 our forces landed in Sicily and after bitter fighting captured the whole island. The Italians were now wavering and when we crossed over to the southern toe of Italy the majority of them realized defeat was inevitable. At a meeting of the Fascist Grand Council in Rome, Mussolini was overthrown and King Victor Emmanuel ordered his imprisonment. Marshal Badoglio headed a new government which surrendered to the Allies. The Germans were enraged at what they considered to be Italian treachery and immediately occupied most of the country. The Germans also managed to free Mussolini and installed him as head of a puppet 'social republican' government. A long and bitter struggle now began for the Italian peninsula. With its many rivers and mountains the country was ideally suited for defence. Our landings at

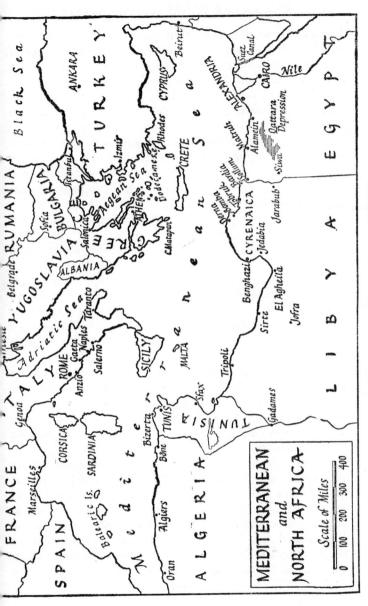

THE MEDITERRANEAN SPHERE OF OPERATIONS

Anzio in an attempt to quicken the advance to Rome were sealed off by the Germans. The bitter German defence of Monte Cassino also held us up for many months. We were not to reach Rome until March 1944.

In May 1942 the Germans launched a massive offensive in the south of Russia. The aim of this offensive was to secure a bridgehead over the Volga at Stalingrad and stop the flow of oil to the Russian armies in the centre and north of the Russian front. The Germans eventually reached Stalingrad and from November to January 1943 tried desperately to take the city. The Russians grimly hung on to part of Stalingrad and were able eventually to encircle the Germans. When the Germans finally surrendered in Stalingrad the Russians found they had taken over 300,000 prisoners. This was a great victory and the Germans were never able to go over to the offensive in Russia again.

The year 1943 was one of almost complete disaster for the Germans. Africa was lost and Italy out of the war. Heavy defeats were suffered in Russia. The only cheering news for the Germans was their invention of the rocket bomber. The first V1, as the rockets came to be called, landed and exploded in London on 13th June 1943. Fortunately our aircraft were able to intercept and shoot down many of these rockets over the channel. Some got through, however, and did much damage. The V1 was also not going to prove the only new weapon the Germans were to unleash against us. We were just beginning to perfect our defence against the V1 when the V2 arrived. The V2 was a frightening weapon. The speed of the rocket was such that it could not be intercepted by our fighter aircraft nor shot down by anti-aircraft fire. Its large container of high explosive caused immense damage. Although we heavily bombed Peenemunde on the Baltic where the V2 was made, the Germans managed to maintain a supply of them to the launching sites in the low countries. The menace of the V2 did not end until we captured these sites a few months after the Normandy landings.

The Normandy Landings

In the spring of 1944 British and American forces in England began to prepare for a knockout blow in the west against Germany. Hitler had for long been boasting about his 'west wall', which, it was claimed, made German occupied France impregnable. We were determined, however, to avenge the defeats of 1940 in France and many hoped a second front against Germany would speedily bring about her total collapse.

Our preparations for landing in France were carefully made over many months and included an attempt to delude the Germans into thinking they would take place in the area of the Straits of Dover. By our bombing of centres in this area the Germans became convinced this was the objective. The chosen coast was, in actual fact, in Normandy—the thirty miles of coast stretching westward from Caen. After heavy naval and air bombardment of German defensive positions we made our landings on 6th June 1944. We quickly established a bridge-head, and while British troops held a strong German counter-attack round Caen the Americans fanned out towards the Loire. We were rapidly building up our strength and the Germans realized each day was vital to them. In August they launched a massive offensive through Falaise designed to split the British and American armies and eventually drive us individually back into the sea. This German army made a deep penetration but we were able to nip them off and the 'Falaise pocket' became another Stalingrad. Paris was liberated, and by November we were threatening the Ruhr and had cleared all France and Belgium of the enemy.

The end of the war seemed imminent but our attempt with airborne units at Arnhem to seize a crossing over the Rhine met with failure. The Germans were also to make one last great effort in the west to delay defeat. In December a hastily improvised army under General Runstedt attacked in the Ardennes and advanced over fifty miles. It was through the

The Second World War 1939-1945

Ardennes that the German army staged its victorious offensive against France in 1940 and Hitler boasted Paris would be reoccupied by the new year. The offensive was finally held, and the losses in men and arms inflicted on the Germans ensured they would be unable to make any protracted stand in the west.

Throughout 1944 the Russians advanced rapidly and by the beginning of 1945 were in East Prussia and Pomerania. At the same time as our forces crossed the Rhine the Russians were crossing the Oder. The war was now clearly over and Germany defeated. The Nazis, unfortunately, still remained in power and determined on resistance to the end even if this meant utter destruction and disaster for Germany. Berlin was besieged by the Russians, and Hitler and Goebbels met their ends there. At the beginning of May a German Government in Kiel under Admiral Doenitz finally surrendered unconditionally to the Allies.

THE DEFEAT OF JAPAN

Japan now remained the last of the Axis powers still in the war. In October 1944 the Americans had won a great naval victory near the Philippines and in the spring of 1945 occupied Okinawa and Iwojima. In May 1945 British forces occupied Rangoon and cleared Burma of the Japanese. Despite these successes it appeared likely that the war in the east would drag on for many months. The Japanese army was still formidable and huge areas of Asia were under Japanese control. On 6th August 1945, however, the Americans dropped the first atom bomb on Hiroshima; nearly the whole town was destroyed and there were hundreds of thousands of casualties. Russia chose this moment to declare war on Japan and invaded Manchuria and Korea. On the 9th August a second atomic bomb was dropped on Nagasaki. Japan had no answer to this horrifying new weapon and on the 10th August surrendered unconditionally.

READING LIST

The Second World War 1939–1945, Major-General J. F. C. Fuller (Eyre & Spottiswoode).

The Struggle for Europe, Chester Wilmot (Collins).

The Second World War Vols I–VII, Winston S. Churchill (Cassell).

Chapter Eight

INTERNATIONAL RELATIONS
SINCE 1945

We have already described in our first chapter how at the end
of the First World War there was a short-lived period of great
optimism for peace and international co-operation. This feeling of optimism we said is common to the immediate period
following all big wars. In 1945 the Second World War ended
with the defeat and unconditional surrender of Germany and
Japan, and a similar jubilant period of optimism about the
future began. The 1939–1945 war it was felt really could be
described as a war to end wars. The Fascist dictatorships—
Germany, Italy and Japan—had all been defeated. Relations
between the Allies were believed to be good, and the Soviet
Union was popular in the west as the country who had broken
the back of the German forces.[1] It was felt a great and lasting
era of peace and international co-operation had been ushered
in—the enemies now were disease, malnutrition, ignorance
and low production; and these should be jointly tackled in the
same spirit that had brought about the defeat of the Fascist
powers. In 1919 hopes for peace had been placed in the League

---

[1] Passages such as the following, which read strangely now, were common
in books about Russia published towards the end of the war:

'Ever since the aggressors were halted before Moscow, the world has received almost daily evidence of the fighting strength, technical skill and
magnificent staying power of the Soviet people. The admiration of the
British people for their Soviet allies has grown steadily. This admiration
and the Russian realisation that Britain was its first comrade-in-arms will
itself be mighty factors in the future relations of our two countries.'

Building Peace out of War, Chapter II. 'Britain and the U.S.S.R.' P.E.P.
1944.

of Nations. In 1945 it was felt the newly formed United Nations Organization would provide the means for the nations co-operatively tackling the world's social problems and maintaining peace.

How different from this was the mood of only three years later. By the end of 1947 western suspicions of Russia's intentions were rapidly growing, and to many people in the democracies Russia seemed as much a menace to peace as did Germany before the war. From 1948 the western democracies began to look to their security again after the initial post-war disarmament. The United Nations Organization was still regarded as the best means of bringing about better international understanding and all hope in the Organization was not jettisoned, but it was felt defensive safeguards must be sought in case suspicions about Russia's intentions were proved correct. By 1948 the world seemed to be splitting increasingly into two armed camps—Russia and her Communist satellites on the one hand and the democracies on the other. Since 1945 the world has seen a developing war of ideas between these two sides to win the allegiance of the uncommitted and, in the case of Russian propaganda, to sow dissension in the population of the democracies. In the Far East, where spheres of influence have not been as clearly demarcated as in other parts of the world, this 'cold war' has sometimes developed into a 'shooting war'—for instance in Korea and French Indo-China.

In this last chapter of the book we want to follow the story of international affairs from 1945 to the Korean truce of July 1953. We shall trace the decline of the unrealistic optimism of 1945, based on the idea that because the Fascist powers had been defeated all would now be well in the field of international relations, and the growth of a more realistic approach in the west based on the concept of making every endeavour to maintain peace and improve relations with the Communist world while at the same time building up the west's defensive strength against possible aggression.

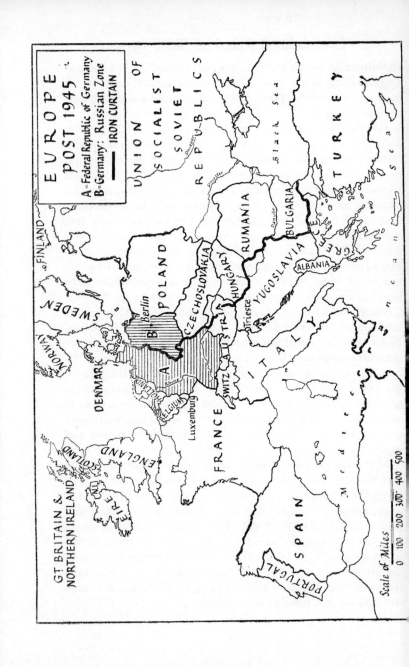

EUROPE
POST 1945

A = Federal Republic of Germany
B = Germany: Russian Zone
━━━ IRON CURTAIN

UNION OF SOVIET SOCIALIST REPUBLICS

FINLAND

SWEDEN

NORWAY

DENMARK

Berlin

POLAND

B

A

Rhine

CZECHOSLOVAKIA

HOLLAND

BELGIUM

Luxemburg

SWITZ

AUSTRIA

HUNGARY

RUMANIA

Danube

YUGOSLAVIA

Trieste

BULGARIA

ALBANIA

GREECE

Black Sea

TURKEY

Aegean Sea

GT. BRITAIN &
NORTHERN IRELAND

SCOTLAND

N. I.

EIRE

ENGLAND

FRANCE

ITALY

SPAIN

PORTUGAL

Mediterranean Sea

Dnieper

Dniester

Scale of Miles
0 100 200 300 400 500

United Nations Organization

On 14th August 1941, at a famous meeting on a battleship in mid-Atlantic, Churchill and Roosevelt had defined the common principles upon which they hoped a new world would be based after the war. The eight points they established became known as 'The Atlantic Charter.'

In 1943 the tide of war against the Axis powers began to turn in favour of the Allies. As soon as it became obvious that victory was now only a matter of time, discussion began among Allied statesmen about the formation of a new organization for international co-operation to take the place of the discredited League of Nations. The idea of a United Nations Organization was discussed by the 'big three'—Churchill, Roosevelt and Stalin—at their Yalta meeting, and at Dumbarton Oaks in America in 1944 representatives of the Allies drew up the draft constitution of the Organization.

In the closing months of the war the formation of the Organization was energetically begun. Even as early as this, however, signs of future trouble between east and west were already apparent and the suspicions of some had already been aroused by a number of Russian actions. For instance, in the former enemy territories she had occupied Russia had done her utmost to place in power puppet Communist Parties without consulting the people in these countries or her Allies. Despite such events, however, people in the west remained very optimistic about the future of international relations and it was genuinely believed that the new Organization would be a success.

The basic idea underlying the United Nations Organization was that the wartime co-operation of the Allies could be continued in years of peace. The aim of the Organization was to secure international co-operation for good relations between the countries of the world and for the solving of major world problems. The meeting-place of the Organization was to be Lake Success in America. The structure of the Organization consisted of a number of different organs as follows:

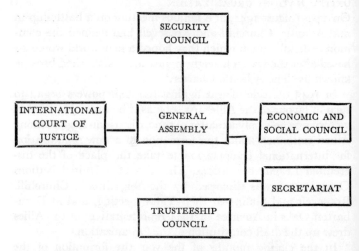

(a.) GENERAL ASSEMBLY: All members of the United Nations Organization may send up to five representatives to the General Assembly. Voting on all matters is on an equal basis, each country, whether large or small, having one vote. A simple majority decides normal questions but for matters of special importance a two-thirds majority of members is required. The Assembly meets once a year. The Assembly has a number of functions—it is the means of keeping all members in touch with U.N.O's work, it is meant to be an active body in promoting international co-operation, and also controls the work of the Trusteeship Council (see below) and U.N.O.'s budget as well as electing people to the various other branches of the Organization.

(b.) SECURITY COUNCIL: The Security Council was designed primarily as the instrument of the big powers in U.N.O. Five permanent members were decided upon in 1945—Britain, America, Russia, France and China (Chiang Kai-shek China). Six non-permanent members would also sit and these would be elected by the General Assembly for a period of two years. Voting would be decided by a majority of seven out of the eleven members and this seven must include all the big five. Each of the big five on the Council had, then, what we call a veto power. Russia had insisted at the Yalta Conference on the veto power being included in U.N.O. and this meant she could stop any measure being passed even if all the other ten members of the Council were in favour. It was intended that the Security Council should be the watch-dog on peace of the United Nations Organization. It is laid down in the constitution of U.N.O. that its main functions are, to investigate and take action about any matter that appears to be threatening peace, to recommend the admission of new members to U.N.O. and to try and regulate world production of armaments.

(c.) ECONOMIC AND SOCIAL COUNCIL: Eighteen countries are elected by the General Assembly to sit on the Economic and Social Council for a period of three years. Decisions of the Council are reached by simple majorities. The work of the Council consists in making studies and recommendations on world economic and social matters. The decisions of the Council are implemented by various subsidiary bodies such as U.N.E.S.C.O. (United Nations Educational, Scientific and Cultural Organization). The purpose of U.N.E.S.C.O. according to its constitution is, 'to contribute to peace and security by promoting collaboration among the nations through education, science and culture in order to further universal respect for justice, for the rule of law, and for the human rights and fundamental freedoms which are affirmed for the peoples of the world, without distinction of race, sex, language, or religion by the Charter of the United Nations.' The work of U.N.E.S.C.O. is divided among a number of commissions; for instance, there are commissions covering Human Rights and the status of women.

(d.) TRUSTEESHIP COUNCIL: This Council consists of all those countries administering trust territories and an equal number of countries not administering trust territories and elected by the General Assembly. The Council's job is to ensure that all trust territories are being developed in the interest of the people living in them.

(*e.*) INTERNATIONAL COURT OF JUSTICE: Fifteen judges, all being citizens of different states, are elected to serve in the International Court of Justice by the General Assembly and Security Council. The period of office of these judges is nine years and they are eligible for re-election. The main task of the Court is to help in maintaining peace by adjudicating in the disputes between members of U.N.O. and thus to build up a universally accepted system of international law. The Court meets at The Hague in Holland.

(*f.*) SECRETARIAT: Obviously a large organization such as U.N.O. requires a good deal of administrative work, and a permananent Secretary-General and his staff attend to this. The Secretary-General is appointed by the General Assembly on the recommendation of the Security Council. As well as being U.N.O.'s chief administrative officer the Secretary-General is empowered to bring before the Security Council for discussion any matter which he considers to threaten peace. He is also reponsible for the compilation of U.N.O.'s annual report.

Having outlined the main organs of U.N.O. we must now comment on its successes and failures in action.

HAS U.N.O. FAILED?

U.N.O. was intended to be the instrument for promoting universal peace all over the world, but it cannot be claimed that it has been entirely successful. It is true that since 1945 U.N.O. has had a number of successes in bringing peace to several world trouble-spots. In 1946 it effected the peaceful withdrawal of French and British troops from Syria and the Lebanon. In 1946 Iran appealed to the Security Council about the presence of Russian troops in her northern provinces and Russia withdrew her forces from this area of Persian Azerbaijan. In 1947 a special committee of U.N.O. did good work

Has U.N.O. Failed?

in ending border incidents between Greece, Bulgaria, Yugoslavia and Albania. In the same year U.N.O. managed to bring an end to hostilities between the Dutch and nationalists in Indonesia. In the same year, largely owing to the hard work of Count Bernadotte, her special envoy, U.N.O. brought about an uneasy truce in Jerusalem where bitter fighting had been taking place between Israeli and Jordan forces.[1] In 1948 a dispute broke out between the new British dominions of India and Pakistan over the possession of a mixed Hindu, Moslem territory called Kashmir, and this dispute developed into actual fighting in Kashmir. A special commission under Sir Owen Dixon was sent out by U.N.O. and in January 1949 a cease-fire was announced and the first steps were soon taken in the demilitarization of Kashmir in order that a plebiscite could be held.

U.N.O. has also done excellent work in fields other than mediation in trouble-spots. U.N.O. has been very active through its various organizations, such as the World Food and Agricultural Organization, in attacking world problems such as those of the under-developed areas, poverty, malnutrition and illiteracy, and in stimulating cultural exchanges between countries. Such problems as malnutrition are really fundamental to mankind's future happiness and U.N.O. has taken energetic measures in setting about tackling them co-operatively.[2]

Since 1945, however, in spite of these successes of U.N.O., we have seen the growth of suspicion and bad relations between

---

[1] Count Folke Bernadotte, a member of the Swedish Royal Family, was later tragically killed while engaged on duties connected with the supervision of the cease-fire.

[2] Even before the war it is believed only one in three human beings in the world received enough food to maintain health. Because of malnutrution infant mortality was very high in many parts of the world. Even in comparatively developed countries such as Roumania and Chile 189 and 225 infants respectively died in their first year of life out of every 1,000 born in 1939. The comparative figure for New Zealand was 32 per 1,000. World food production will have to be substantially increased if everyone in the world is to have enough to eat.

WORLD POPULATION 1957

JAPAN 90 m.

CHINA - 590 m.

RUSSIA 210 m.

E. EUROPE 90 m.

WEST EUROPE 320 m.
BRITAIN 51
FRANCE 43
GERMANY 70
ITALY 48

ARABS 80 m.

AFRICA 160 m.

SOUTHERN ASIA - 760 m.
INDIA & PAKISTAN 460
220
INDONESIA 80

AUSTRALIA & NEW ZEALAND 12 m.

CANADA 16 m.

U.S.A. 170 m.

LATIN AMERICA 180 m.
BRAZIL 60

Has U.N.O. Failed?

Russia and the western powers. By 1948 the high optimism of the summer of 1945 had largely disappeared. In many people, in fact, it has been replaced by a deep depression concerning the chances for peace. It is unrealistic to hold U.N.O. responsible for this deterioration in the relations of the wartime Allies. It is rather the result of east and west being unable to genuinely give and take in the meetings of the Security Council. It is not U.N.O. that is at fault, but the great powers who have failed to make her institutions work in the way the optimists of 1945 hoped for.

THE SPLIT BETWEEN EAST AND WEST

When the war ended in 1945 Britain along with her other western Allies started a rapid process of disarmament. The problems of reconstruction were now given first priority, and a reduction of the huge labour force in the armed services or involved in their provisioning was quickly begun. At the end of the war Britain had 5,100,000 people in her armed forces. By 1946 this had been reduced to 2,233,000 and a year later was down to 1,427,000. The west looked forward to close co-operation with Russia and could see no purpose in maintaining these large wartime forces.

By the end of 1947, however, the early hopes of friendship with Russia had not been realized, and suspicions concerning Russia's intentions began to grow. Russia, for a start, had never disarmed at the end of the war to the extent that the west had done. Two years after the end of the war her forces were estimated to be still well over 3,000,000. By 1947, also, the beginnings of a propaganda war—the cold war—against the west had appeared. At the end of the war Russia had dissolved her old organization of world Communist Parties, the Comintern, and founded a new organization to direct the activities of Communist Parties abroad called the Cominform. Through Cominform control of the Communist Parties Russia did her utmost to disrupt democratic institutions abroad. In Italy and France, where at the end of the war

Communist Parties were very strong, Russia hoped that Communists would soon be in control of the new republican régimes that had appeared. By the end of 1947 Russia had also got a firm hold over eastern Europe. Poland, Roumania, Hungary, Bulgaria and Albania had all become Communist satellites, and in 1948 Czechoslovakia was to follow suit. Until Tito's break with the Cominform in 1948 Yugoslavia was also considered a Russian satellite. In these satellites opposition to the Communist régimes was gradually stamped out, monarchists, liberals and socialists being executed, imprisoned and intimidated. Russia's use of the veto on the Security Council was on many occasions merely obstructive and gave the impression that she had no real intention of making U.N.O. work. By the end of 1947, then, a decided split had appeared between Russia and the democracies. The western powers began to realize that although every effort must be made to make U.N.O. work security must be sought outside it in case bad relations with Russia should deteriorate into war.

WESTERN ECONOMIC CO-OPERATION

Before any large-scale rearmament could take place, however, the democracies had to recover economically from the effect of the war. The destruction of the war years, German occupation, low production, and, as in the case of Britain, the selling of foreign investments, brought the countries of Europe against serious economic problems at the end of the war. Between 1945 and 1947 those countries like Britain who relied on a large number of imports to maintain their living standards suffered from what economists call adverse balance of payments. That is, they had not been selling enough to pay for the goods being imported and this excess of imports over exports was only paid for in the following three ways.

(a.) By using up gold reserves.

(b.) By borrowing reconstruction loans from America—the

largest being the American loan of three-and-a-half billion dollars to Britain.

(*c.*) By obtaining help from the United Nations Relief and Rehabilitation Association which was largely subsidized by the American Government. This system of living by a mixture of using up capital, borrowing and charity obviously could not be continued indefinitely and the bad winter of 1947 with its fuel shortages brought Europe close to economic collapse.

Energetic measures were necessary if western Europe was to become solvent and be in a position to build up her military power. America had meanwhile been watching the spread of Russian power in eastern Europe with apprehension and by 1947 was very suspicious of Russian intentions. America realized that to leave a weak and economically demoralized Europe would only be playing into Russia's hands. America had turned her back on the pre-war policy of isolation and had joined U.N.O. By 1947 she wished to build up a mutual security system of democracies and realized economic aid would have to be given to help their recovery.

On the 4th June 1947, the American Secretary of State (the equivalent of the British Foreign Minister) General Marshal made an important speech at Harvard University in which he emphasized the necessity of American aid for Europe. This policy of American aid became known as the European Recovery Programme. In 1947 all hope of co-operation with Russia had not been abandoned and Russia and the satellites were actually invited to take part in this plan for close economic co-operation. Russia and her satellites, however, declined this invitation and Russia described this plan as a means of spreading American domination in Europe. On the 3rd April 1948, Congress voted the first sum of money for E.R.P. and decided that six billion dollars should be spent during the first year of the scheme.

Meanwhile the countries of western Europe were not relying on American aid alone. Every country did its utmost to stimulate production and each government to some degree began to plan the use of resources. In Britain a Labour Government was in power and the complex wartime system of economic controls was continued, the coal industry and railway transport being nationalized. Some countries such as Belgium, preferred to allow a greater freedom in their economic life while, as we have already stated, maintaining a certain amount of state direction. But whatever the economic philosophy of the various governments the aim of each was the same—economic health and solvency.

This individual effort, coupled with the benefits of American aid, brought about a great improvement in Europe's economic position. By January 1950 pre-war standards of production had been passed in Britain, France, Belgium and Holland, and even in devastated western Germany production was rapidly improving. When the European Recovery Programme was initiated it was considered Britain would need aid for four years but such was her rate of recovery that she was able to inform America after only eighteen months that no more aid was required. On the 6th April 1948 the Organization for European Co-operation (O.E.E.C.) was formed by sixteen nations, and western Europe has done her utmost since then to achieve an integrated economy.

WESTERN POLITICAL AND MILITARY CO-OPERATION

While Europe was trying to recover from the economic effects of the war and pay her way, the bases of western political co-operation were being laid in the Council of Europe at Strasbourg—a west European parliament where representatives of the democracies could meet and discuss the common problems of Europe. As her economic prospects brightened a beginning was also made in closer military co-operation and rearmament. In March 1948 the Brussels Treaty was signed by Britain, France and the Benelux powers (Belgium, Netherlands and Luxembourg). This treaty laid down a system of mutual defence and military co-operation. On the 4th April 1949, the Brussels Treaty was expanded into the Atlantic Pact

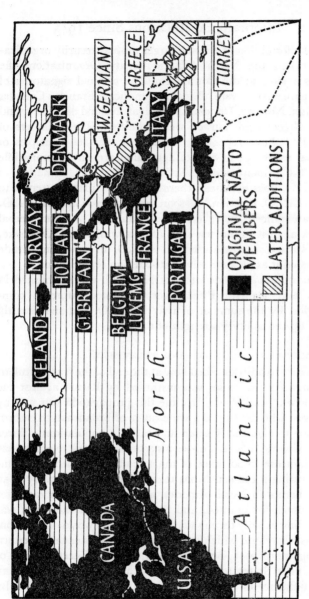

THE ATLANTIC ALLIANCE

and the formation of a much larger mutual security organization called the North Atlantic Treaty Organization—the west's answer to the Cominform. The original signatories of this agreement were Britain, America, France, Canada, Benelux, Norway, Denmark, Portugal, Iceland and Italy, and later Greece and Turkey were admitted. The members of N.A.T.O. have repeatedly reaffirmed that its principles of mutual assistance in case of aggression are not incompatible with the principles of U.N.O., and that the formation of N.A.T.O. does not mean there will be no further attempt to make U.N.O. function. As soon as the formation of N.A.T.O. was announced, however, Russia launched a bitter verbal attack against it and ten days after it was signed, Gromyko, the Russian representative in U.N.O. in a violent tirade described it as an aggressive anti-Russian organization.

The military headquarters of N.A.T.O. was established in Paris and General Eisenhower appointed supreme commander. By the summer of 1953 N.A.T.O. had significantly built up the military strength of the west.

DEVELOPMENT OF RADIO AND TELEVISION

We have already described how at the end of the war a virulent propaganda campaign was instituted by Russia against the democratic way of life. In time this propaganda was met by the west who developed a wide range of broadcasts to eastern Europe to give the Russian and satellite populations a fairer view of world affairs. This seems a suitable point to emphasize the immense importance of the spread of the means of communicating ideas which has taken place since 1945. By 1953 most homes in North America and Europe took a radio set very much for granted, and the possession of radio sets was spreading rapidly throughout the rest of the world. Television, too, is a medium which has come into prominence in western Europe since 1945. Before the war, except for certain parts of the United States, television had not attained a position of any real influence in the world as a means of communication. By

Development of Radio and Television

1953, however, the television set in the United States had reached the same position as the radio and was something taken for granted in most homes. In Britain and a few countries of western Europe it was approaching that position. Britain, for instance, had over four million television sets in use at the end of our period, and this number was increasing rapidly. The assault on illiteracy since the end of the war has also increased the influence of newspapers and the written word in general. The means of influencing men's minds are now widespread and powerful and great responsibility rests with those who control them.

THE FAR EAST

In 1949 events in China were to alter completely the whole balance of power in Asia. In the space of a few months in 1949 the Chinese Communists conquered the country and forced Chiang Kai-shek and a rump government and army to flee the mainland for the island of Formosa. America refused to recognize the Communist Government and continued her support of Chiang Kai-shek, making Formosa a virtual American protectorate. Britain, meanwhile, had recognized the Communist Peking Government. In their approach to the problem of China a substantial divergence in American and British foreign policy was soon evident, Britain favouring the eventual admission of Communist China to the Security Council. At the end of 1953, however, Chiang Kai-shek's representative still sat there.

In Europe by 1948 the line dividing the two worlds—the Iron Curtain—was clear and both sides respected it realizing that encroachments would only lead to war. In the Far East, however, the demarcation line between Communist and non-Communist spheres of influence was not as distinct so early and small 'shooting' wars (as against the cold war in Europe) broke out in some areas. Britain found herself fighting Communist terrorists in Malaya where her ability to demonstrate to the population that she genuinely wished to work towards eventual Malayan dominion status reduced the terrorists by 1953 to a few hounded gangs. In French Indo-China France was not so successful in her fight against Viet Minh Communists and lost the support of a substantial part of the population. The republics of Burma, Indonesia and the Philippines also had difficulty in suppressing Communist risings.

THE KOREAN WAR

Before the end of the war the peninsula of Korea had been a Japanese colony. In 1945 it was occupied in the north by Russian troops and in the south by the Americans. By 1949 all foreign troops had been withdrawn leaving the country split into a North Korean Communist state and a South Korean democracy. On the 25th June South Korea claimed North Korean troops had violated her frontier and a civil war quickly developed. On the 27th June, America summoned a special meeting of the Security Council which declared North Korea an aggressor and ordered her to withdraw to the 38th parallel (the border between the north and south republics). This declaration was made possible by the non-attendance of Russia who had walked out of a meeting of the Security Council in January 1950, and had not yet reappeared. North Korea did not comply with this decision. By July 1950 American troops had landed in Korea to rescue the routed South Korean army and these American forces were quickly joined by British and other United Nations contingents. In August the war became serious with U.N.O. forces hemmed into a tiny triangle of territory around the port of Pusan. In September however, a brilliantly executed landing in central Korea completely changed the position and the North Korean army was encircled and virtually destroyed. After U.N.O. forces had advanced into North Korea, Chinese troops entered the war and the fighting line was eventually stabilized on the 38th parallel where the war dragged on with varying fortunes until 1953.

The Korean War

In 1952 negotiations began with the Communists at Panmunjon to bring the war to an end. When the war broke out the North Koreans had no doubt anticipated a quick and easy victory, but by 1952 it had become obvious that the war had ended in a stalemate. An armistice was eventually concluded in July 1953 leaving the position in Korea roughly what it was before the war had broken out. The Korean war demonstrated to the Communist world an important lesson—the determination of the democracies to withstand aggression wherever it took place and to defend strenuously their sphere of influence.

THE SMALLER COUNTRIES

In this book we have been concerned with the history of the period 1919 to 1953 mainly in terms of the internal history and interactions of the major powers. Many smaller countries, such as Czechoslovakia, have played important parts in this story and have received a fair amount of space. It has not been possible, however, to enter into great detail regarding the economics and politics of these countries in our period. It must not be thought, because of our concentration on the activities of the great powers which have been largely responsible for the pattern of our times, that the valuable work and example on behalf of peace and good will of a number of smaller countries in the post-war years is forgotten. There is an old saying that a happy country has no history and countries such as Sweden (which has kept uninvolved in war for a century and a half) and Switzerland do not often figure in history books. The great powers, however, can 'earn much from the behaviour of these smaller countries who often appear very sensible in their concentration on internal welfare and peaceful dealings with other nations.

READING LIST

A.B.C. of the United Nations and International Organizations, U.N. Association.

The Struggle for Lasting Peace, U.N. Dept., of Public Information.

Britain and the United Nations, H.M.S.O.

Western European Union, Royal Institute of International Affairs.

The West at Bay, B. Ward (Allen & Unwin).

Atlantic Alliance, Royal Institute of International Affairs.

New World Arising, H. Hopkins (Hamilton).

ESSAY QUESTIONS

1. Outline the main provisions of the peace treaties with Germany, Austria, Hungary and Bulgaria at the end of the First World War.

2. In what ways could the peace treaties with the central powers be described as 'vindictive'?

3. What was the idea of mandated territory, and which former enemy territories were defined as mandates?

4. Could Japan be described as having 'climbed down' at the Washington Conference?

5. Why was the Treaty of Lausanne a success?

6. What was the main objective of the League of Nations? Describe briefly its main organs.

CHAPTER II

1. What were the main problems facing the Bolsheviks when they came to power in 1917?

2. Outline the career of either Lenin or Trotsky.

3. The Soviet Union's claim to be a democracy cannot be accepted. Discuss.

4. In what ways did the Russian Communists use education as a means of furthering their aims?

5. To what degree can the citizens of the Soviet Union be said to enjoy religious toleration?

CHAPTER III

1. Show how because of the American system of government Wilson failed in his attempt to get America to join the League.

Essay Questions

2. Describe and comment on the methods of the Republicans in the 'twenties in stimulating private business.

3. Describe how Roosevelt's New Deal policy dealt with the problems of the slump.

4. In 1918 the majority of Americans strongly supported isolationism. In 1945 they were just as strongly convinced of the need for playing an active part in world affairs. Comment.

5. Discuss the position of the negro in American society today.

CHAPTER IV

1. Describe the early difficulties of the Weimar Republic from the abdication of the Kaiser to 1923.

2. Show how Stresemann attempted to improve the position of Germany.

3. Outline the factors which aided the Nazi rise to power in Germany.

4. Show the stages, up to his attack on Poland, by which Hitler obtained the return of German territory lost at Versailles.

5. Mussolini was similar to other Fascist leaders—he was an adventurer interested solely in the enjoyment of political power. Discuss.

6. Describe Japanese aggressions up to the attack on Pearl Harbour.

CHAPTER V

1. Describe the events which led to the formation of the National Government in 1931.

2. What, in your view, were the main mistakes of British foreign policy in the inter-war years?

3. Distinguish between Dominions and Colonies in the British Commonwealth and describe the development in the number of Dominions.

4. Why is the Middle East so important to Britain?

Essay Questions

CHAPTER VI

1. Describe the French search for security in the inter-war years.

2. What reasons were there for the instability of governments in the Third Republic?

CHAPTER VII

1. Outline the main events of the Battle of Britain, August and September, 1940.

2. What do you consider were the major reasons for Hitler's failure to defeat Russia?

3. Describe the campaigns in North Africa up to the German surrender in Tunisia.

4. Describe the Ardennes offensive of December 1944 and account for the German failure.

CHAPTER VIII

1. Describe the six main organs of the United Nations Organization.

2. The failure of U.N.O. to maintain good relations between East and West has obscured the excellent work done by U.N.O. in tackling vital world economic and social problems. Discuss.

3. Describe the formation of the North Atlantic Treaty Organization and give arguments for admitting any other country you feel should be a member of it.

4. The high state of tension in the Far East after 1945 was a result of the Communist and non-Communist worlds having no recognized line to respect dividing their spheres of influence. Discuss.

APPENDICES

(The Preamble)

The High Contracting Parties,

In order to promote international co-operation and to achieve international peace and security;

By the acceptance of obligations not to resort to war;

By the prescription of open, just, and honourable relations between nations;

By the firm establishment of the understandings of international law as the actual rule of conduct among Governments; and

By the maintenance of justice and a scrupulous respect for all treaty obligations in the dealings of organized peoples with one another:
Agree to the Covenant of the League of Nations.

2. THE ATLANTIC CHARTER
(14th August 1941)

The President of the United States and the Prime Minister, Mr. Churchill, representing His Majesty's Government in the United Kingdom, being met together, deem it right to make known certain common principles in the national policies of their respective countries on which they base their hopes for a better future for the world.

1. Their countries seek no aggrandizement, territorial or other.

2. They desire to see no territorial changes that do not

accord with the freely expressed wishes of the peoples concerned.

3. They respect the rights of all peoples to choose the form of Government under which they will live; and they wish to see sovereign rights and self-government restored to those who have been forcibly deprived of them.

4. They will endeavour, with due respect for their existing obligations, to further enjoyment by all states, great or small, victor or vanquished, of access, on equal terms, to the trade and to the raw materials of the world which are needed for their economic prosperity.

5. They desire to bring about the fullest collaboration between all nations in the economic field, with the object of securing for all improved labour standards, economic advancement, and social security.

6. After the final destruction of Nazi tyranny, they hope to see established a peace which will afford to all nations the means of dwelling in safety within their own boundaries, and which will afford assurance that all the men in all the lands may live out their lives in freedom from fear and want.

7. Such a peace should enable all men to traverse the high seas and oceans without hindrance.

8. They believe all of the nations of the world, for realistic as well as spiritual reasons, must come to the abandonment of the use of force. Since no future peace can be maintained if land, sea, or air armaments continue to be employed by nations which threaten or may threaten aggression outside of their frontiers, they believe, pending the establishment of a wider and permanent system of general security, that the disarmament of such nations is essential. They will likewise aid and encourage all other practicable measures which will lighten for peace-loving peoples the crushing burden of armament.

Appendices

(The Preamble)

(Signed by fifty Nations on 26th June, 1945, at the San Francisco Conference)

We the peoples of the United Nations,

Determined to save succeeding generations from the scourge of war, which twice in our lifetime has brought untold sorrow to mankind;

to reaffirm faith in fundamental human rights, in the dignity and worth of the human person, and in the equal rights of men and women of the nations large and small;

to establish conditions under which justice and respect for obligations arising from treaties and other sources of international law can be maintained;

to promote social progress and better standards of life in larger freedom;

to practice tolerance and live together in peace with one another as good neighbours;

to unite our strength to maintain international peace and security;

to ensure, by the acceptance of principles and by the institution of methods, that armed force shall not be used, save in the common interest;

to employ international machinery for the promotion of the economic and social advancement of all peoples:

have resolved to combine our efforts to accomplish these aims,

have agreed to the present Charter of the United Nations, and do hereby establish an international organization to be known as the United Nations.

INDEX

(N.B. *The names of the Great Powers, which occur continuously throughout the book, are not included in the Index.*)

Index

Index

Index